Charlotte Maria Pepys

A Journey on a Plank from Kiev to Eaux-Bonnes

1859. Vol. 2

Charlotte Maria Pepys

A Journey on a Plank from Kiev to Eaux-Bonnes
1859. Vol. 2

ISBN/EAN: 9783744754033

Printed in Europe, USA, Canada, Australia, Japan

Cover: Foto ©Andreas Hilbeck / pixelio.de

More available books at **www.hansebooks.com**

EAUX-BONNES.

FROM

KIEV TO EAUX-BONNES.

1859.

BY LADY CHARLOTTE PEPYS.

IN TWO VOLUMES.
VOL. II.

LONDON:
HURST AND BLACKETT, PUBLISHERS,
SUCCESSORS TO HENRY COLBURN,
13, GREAT MARLBOROUGH STREET.
1860.
The right of Translation is reserved.

CONTENTS OF VOL. II.

CHAPTER I.

Departure from Frankfort—Hearing Russian Voices and Accents—"Alexandre"—"Utrom"—"Run" to secure Places—Defence against Intruders—Oos Junction—A Family Party—M. Clodion—Mlle. Platpied. . . 1

CHAPTER II.

Arrival at Kehl—Bridge—Strasburg—Letters—The Cathedral—Erwin of Steinbach—Guttemburg—London Emissary—Rothschild's Emissary—Colmar—Historical Hangings—Vosges Mountains—Oberlin—Jeanne d'Arc—Mülhausen—La Chapelle—Group in Buffet—The War—Milanese Charity—Franche Comté—Sequania—Burgundy—Besançon, formerly Vesontio—"B. and V."—Montbeliard and Cuvier—Montbard and Buffon—The Doubs—Its Course—Grotte d'Oselle—Cardinal Roland and Alexander III.—The Rhone does *not* flow towards Paris—Impressions of Besançon—Its Trade—An Old-fashioned Town and Hotel—Departure—Café de la Gare—Reflections—Place of Waiting 21

CHAPTER III.

Dejeûner—" Waiting"—Dôle—Our Line of March—Dijon—Recollections—Wounded in the Train—Hôtel du Parc—" Walter "—" M. l'Anglais "—Hôtel de l'Europe—The Old "Fustiness"—River Travelling—Fellow-travellers—The Rhône — Perrache—Vienne—Valence—Montélimart— Orange—French Popes—Men of Limousin—Avignon—Luxury of Climate—Recollections—Departure for Cette — Austrian Prisoners — Tarascon — St. Martha—Nimes—Montpellier 48

CHAPTER IV.

Cette—Wounded Officer—Agde—Béziers—Maguelonne—Panama Hats—The War—Narbonne—Narbonensis—M. Philippe—Mme. Philippe— His Adventures—Her Adventures — Their Consolations — Madame Lawless — Corbières—Hits—Caunes Quarries—Last sight of M. and Mme. Philippe—Arrival at Toulouse—Raymond—Church Service—Claims of Toulouse to Interest—Impressions—The Calas Family—Obelisk—Aspect of Streets and Houses —The House Opposite—Apology for a Fiction . 74

CHAPTER V.

The Little House with Green Shutters . . . 92

CHAPTER VI.

Departure from Toulouse—Journey to Tarbes—Country—Froissart—Tarbes—Ascent—Rencontre—Pau—Ascent to Eaux-Bonnes—Arrival at Louvie—Arrival at Eaux-Bonnes—Impressions—Red Rooms—Description—The Day in Pau—Arrival of the Party—Life at Eaux-Bonnes —Fête Day—Games—Friends—Summer's Last Days—Expeditions — Russian Tea — Autumnal Weather — Removal to Pau—Conclusion 216

VERSES AND TRANSLATIONS FROM THE RUSSIAN.

The Pine	253
Clouds	254
The Angel	255
A Sail	256
A Wish	257
The Rock and the Wave	259
The Thorne-Staffe	261
The Dove	263
Avignon Cemetery	268
The Fount—Separation	270

JOURNEY ON A PLANK

FROM

KIEV TO EAUX-BONNES.

CHAPTER I.

Departure from Frankfort—Hearing Russian Voices and Accents—" Alexandre "—" Utrom "—" Run " to secure Places—Defence against Intruders—Oos Junction—A Family Party—M. Clodion—Mlle. Platpied.

AT last, at last, I had taken opium, and smoked cigarettes, Russian cigarettes, so diligently, that my neuralgia gave way, and, feeling in consequence stronger, I decided that if the next day's post did not bring the letter,

I must give up this last link, and go on to Strasburg the next day. And we did so. Just as we were starting, the master of the hotel received a telegram, to inquire if we were still there. He replied that we were going by the express then starting. We travelled through much heat and dust to Heidelberg, and were very glad to get out there, to seek a quiet hotel in which to dine. I had a little room, looking on to a Piazza and garden deliciously shady—quite a *rest*. While I was alone there, I heard some one speaking next door, and the accent immediately attracted me. French was the language; but there was something *not* French in the way of utterance, and in the tone of voice—something deeper and larger —Russian, in short. There was no possibility of not hearing what was said; and I am sure the speakers did not mind who heard the arrangements they were making for driving out before the late dinner—" evidently *à-la-carte,*" said I to myself; "another national characteristic I know well." Presently the name "Alexandre" arrested my attention; and then the carriage being drawn up, I saw a lady and gentleman of very Russian exterior enter it and drive off. If that gentleman were Alexander, he was very unlike the Alexander to whom that name must in my ideas pre-eminently belong.

Though they were gone, I soon became aware that theirs were only some of the Russian voices I had heard: others were still conversing on the piazza. I listened with pleasure to the sounds, though they were now too far off for me to hear anything but the national rich tones and soft accents. Soon the French glided into Russian; and a young, very young lady ran past as if to give some message. I fancied that something in her hair, foot, or features would have told me she was Russian, even without the magical word with which she turned round to the group she had quitted, as if to reply to a remark of theirs ere entering the Hôtel—that word was " utrom "—" in the morning ;" and how many plans for pleasant days, and busy days, did it not recall ! I felt myself at once in the midst of that far-away household, listening to plans for hunting, sketching, riding, fishing, travelling, studying—in short, that little word enters so constantly into human plans, that it is not surprising it should have been one of the first heard, and best remembered. An eager, hopeful, glowing little word—not always, however, associated with pleasant undertakings. For instance, how often will a doctor not pronounce upon a case, nor try a new remedy, till he has seen his patient "in the morning." How many a lesson over which we have stupefied ourselves at night has to be begun all over again "in the morning;" and how many bright plans, that look to our eager eyes feasible enough and sure of success at night, are coolly laid upon the shelf, to be talked over "in the morning." And we know that the patient will look worse, the lesson be entirely forgotten, "in the morning,"—and the bright plans, like glaciers after sunset, all the darker and colder-looking for the sunset-glow that had surrounded them with rosy beauty. "Utrom" (it suited the fair girl who had uttered it) looked at me, and I looked at her and her little yelping dog—not a "Beauty"—and wished I dared to tell her how much her one word of Russian had suggested to me. How little "utrom" guessed the pleasure she had given to me! How little "Diamond" knew the injury he had done to Sir Isaac Newton!

That was a pleasant day, that 27th of July, resting in the little room looking out upon the Piazza, and the shady garden, and the green hills. I could not see the Castle — nor had Florence or Godfrey been able to do so; for having been afraid of changing too many notes into gold, they had to get more changed here, and I fear saw little else beside the banker's den; while I was quietly and comfortably enjoying my repose. The train came before we quite expected it, and we had almost to *run* to get places. Florence would not leave me, and I could not go fast; nevertheless, we succeeded at last, and were glad to take our seats after such a race. We had the carriage to ourselves part of the way.

Florence was very much amused at my taking no notice at all of some poor man who presented himself at the door; and he, seeing the entrance barred by a prostrate and apparently unconscious figure, retreated, visibly alarmed. At Oos Junction, however, the train from Baden-Baden came in, and brought plenty of passengers to fill all vacant places. Four were shown into our carriage; however, I still lay up, as we were only two. The party now entering occupied our attention not a little during the rest of our journey to Kehl. It was composed of a gentleman, whom we will call M. Clodion (I like good old names, but Pharamond is too ugly) — a fine handsome woman, Madame Clodion, *née Princesse Comnène* (I am sure her card must run in that strain), and a pretty, delicate little girl of about eleven years old. I give her the name of Zoe, and her governess that of Mlle. Platpied. The latter two interested me the most at first; for the poor little girl was in a sad state—quite a patient for Eaux-Bonnes, I feared. Every instant she exclaimed, "Je veux cracher!" and immediately dyed a handkerchief crimson; then she cried, and trembled, and finally dropped asleep—waking up bewildered, and spreading out her hands, as if uncertain where she was. The poor mother seemed much alarmed, and wept quietly, while the child slept, leaning against her. I am sure she was a very Zoe (life) to her mother, that little maiden. Mlle Platpied had one of those peculiar constructions that seem to sit down upon springs, the vibration whereof must give affected little rebounds to the whole upper person. She appeared to me to be occupied with everything rather than with her pupil; but as she was laden with boxes and bags innumerable, the three hats and parasols, and the child's mantle and gloves, she could not do much more than attend to these articles, and to five immense bouquets with which she was also charged.

These bouquets, by-the-bye, were, if not the first, certainly one of the most prominent subjects of conversation during our journey; that is to say, as soon as the little girl's ailments abated. And here I must protest that I had not the slightest intention of trying to read a page of family history; but when one assists at a rehearsal of a scene like this, one hardly feels bound to secresy. M. Clodion, a small and timid-looking dark man, asked

Mlle. Platpied to show him the bouquets. She showed him one or two, throwing them down again on the seat beside her; but he was not satisfied—he wanted to see the one which she retained in her hand, and from which hung out a beautiful little green sprig of some herb, "romantic or aromatic," and this she would not show him, taking her cue all the while from the piercing eyes of Madame Clodion, who appeared greatly to enjoy his discomfiture. He was silent for a few minutes, but soon renewed the attack. This time he was left in perfect silence—without any answer at all; and the two ladies, leaning over the little invalid, began a whispered conversation, interrupted by little fits of giggling laughter. Thus foiled, the poor man sunk back into his corner.

The child was asleep, and he suggested that she had better have a cloak put over her. "Ne la tourmentez pas!" was the reply. He then endeavoured to pull up the window near her, but was peremptorily desired to desist. He tried to converse in a low voice with Madame Clodion; whereupon she looked exceedingly exhausted, and, closing her eyes, declared that she had a tremendous headache. Baffled at all points, the meek Clodion again had recourse to Mlle Platpied and her bouquets, leaving his wife to slumber, if she liked it. This, however, was not, I hoped, very necessary to her; for she was evidently alive to all that went on; and Mlle. Platpied apparently thought so, for she continued the same style of answer to whatever was suggested by M. Clodion, if she thought it worthy of an answer at all. In fact, she played the part of sycophant to her haughty mistress so admirably that I could scarcely believe her to be sincere.

At last, weary of being browbeaten, M. Clodion had the folly to ask what they were talking about and looking at, when their whispered conversations began again.

"It's Bernard riding by the side of the train," said Mme. Clodion, as she would have answered a fool or an idiot.

"Did you see him this morning?" he replied; "and did Zoe see her little friend?"

"Taisez vous donc, imbecile!" replied his gentle wife; and perhaps she was not far wrong, for they had informed us that all the child's illness had been caused by "l'émotion de quitter ses amis."

The young lady was now awake, and appeared not to lose a syllable of what was said about herself and other matters. She was much better, and they gave her some *bon-bons*, and began to talk about the causes of her attack, which M. Clodion attributed to a five o'clock dinner. This fact he communicated to Florence, with whom he had already begun to converse. His wife, hearing the statement, replied indignantly that "It was the emotion!—one could not quit one's friends without feeling emotion;" and then indignation giving way to sorrow, real or feigned, her eyes sought and met a sympathetic glance from Mlle. Platpied, over the bouquets, and closed languidly.

The poor child was again suffering severely, or bitter might have been the war of words that ensued ; but she claimed the attention of all. Florence gave her some salts, and the mother thanked her, speaking to us for the first time directly. I asked Mlle. Platpied, aside, if the child was liable to these attacks; and she replied, "Oh, no; there were no fears for her chest, but violent crying had caused her to bleed from the nose and throat."

"Poor little thing!" I replied, "one can see that she is in a very nervous, excited state."

I spoke low that the child might not hear me; but in vain—for the mother replied eagerly—

"Oh, yes—she is excessively nervous, excessively nervous, poor little pet!"

Mlle. Platpied, by-the-way, was so fearfully affected, that even when we stopped at a station, and the child asked for a glass of water, she could not raise anything like a voice to call with, out of her ponderous proportions, but whined out,—" Ein glas wasser" adding, in a yet more lamentable tone, "Mann hört nicht; es ist krank das Kind." The father handed a florin; and I, eagerly seizing it, touched her up without ceremony, saying, " Donnez donc, Mlle., et quelqu'un vous apportera de l'eau?" My words were verified by the immediate arrival of a refreshing glass of water, which much revived the little invalid.

Re-assured by seeing her calm and cheerful again, all seemed for a short time to go on smoothly. Florence amused the papa—the mamma and the child exchanged caresses and endearing words, and Mlle. Platpied ogled her bouquets, about which, as also about her own movements and plans, she affected a considerable air of mystery, replying to every question of M. Clodion's by the oracular words,

"C'est possible, il en a été question; cela se pourrait."

I hoped it was her marriage, or her departure, or anything which would remove her from her position near that interesting child, whose education already seemed likely to prove a thorny path, beset with dangers, from the perpetual recurrence of divisions between the parents; and Mlle. Platpied, instead of taking no part in these disputes, appeared to delight in fomenting them.

The present serene state of affairs could not last. The child dropped asleep; the father wished her to put on a cloak, as it was getting late; and when this proposal was received with an annihilating look, he desisted only for a few minutes, and then drew up the window; whereupon the lady declared again that she had a tremendous headache, and threw herself back in the seat.

"Est-ce aussi de l'emotion?" said he, pointedly. And then commenced a scene worthy of the pen of a Dumas or a Féval—mine is quite inadequate to describe how M. Clodion drew near to Mme. Clodion, saying that he had something to say to her; and how she immediately affected sleep or deafness, opening her eyes the next moment, and whispering again with Mlle. Platpied; how he retreated into himself, but quickly returned to the charge, directly he discovered the subterfuge. If he caught her with her eyes open, and she had no time to shut them, she looked beyond him, as if something very interesting were written on the grey cloth of the carriage; or out of the window, or at one of us, as if she saw us for the first time. But if she had time she closed her eyes, murmuring, "Do let me be in peace when I am so ill! Cannot you understand that my head aches violently?"

He was very imprudent, and renewed his attempts continually. At last she deigned to reply; and her reply excited him to speak less cautiously; whereupon she entreated him to remember the presence of strangers—if her poor wishes for peace had no weight with him, he might at least consider that it was "inconvenant" to drag their misfortunes before people who were totally unknown to them both. It was hard enough, Heaven knew, to have such a destiny; but all the world need not perceive it, if he had but common courtesy and good breeding.

The little girl was now wide awake; and her father put on her cloak—for the excited lady had let down the glass. This caused a fresh outburst.

"De grâce, ménagez-moi en presence de cette enfant; pour moi je ne dis pas, mais pour cette enfant!"

Our arrival at Kehl caused Florence to say something to me about a carriage; and M. Clodion told his child to keep on her cloak— (she had already, apt pupil, thrown it off, with an appealing look to her mother)—for that she would be in the omnibus directly.

"En omnibus! mais je n'irai pas en omnibus! je n'y suis pas habituée, moi!" exclaimed the indignant fair one; and ceasing to be a "femme incomprise," she became a practical "Hausfrau;" for by the time my slow exit from the train was accomplished, and I was placed on a bundle of cloaks, under the wall, to wait for a carriage — she had secured the only one, put her Platpied and her Zoe into it, was recognizing and claiming her luggage, and elbowing her slower husband out of the way, at the barrier.

We were not sorry to see no more of this calm and happy ménage! Mlle. Platpied was indeed seen walking the next day in Strasburg, but her companion on that occasion was certainly not a pupil.

CHAPTER II.

Arrival at Kehl—Bridge—Strasburg—Letters—The Cathedral—Erwin of Steinbach—Guttemburg—London Emissary—Rothschild's Emissary—Colmar—Historical Hangings—Vosges Mountains—Oberlin—Jeanne d'Arc—Mülhausen—La Chapelle—Group in Buffet—The War—Milanese Charity—Franche Comté—Sequania—Burgundy—Besançon, formerly Vesontio—"B. and V."—Moutbeliard and Cuvier—Montbard and Buffon—The Doubs—Its Course—Grotte d'Oselle—Cardinal Roland and Alexander III.—The Rhone does *not* flow towards Paris—Impressions of Besançon—Its Trade—An Old-fashioned Town and Hotel—Departure—Café de la Gare —Reflections—Place of Waiting.

WE obtained a carriage at length, and went over the bridge at Strasburg. It is extraordinary that this should still be necessary; however, the railway bridge is now nearly completed—and the men were working at it late that night, between 9 and 10 o'clock; so I suppose the Emperor has expressed the same surprise at its not being accomplished yet.

Strasburg gave me a strange nervous sensation, from the pitch of its roofs, suggesting inevitable destruction to any one who should venture upon them. In the moonlight they looked quite fearfully suggestive of imminent danger. We went to the "Hôtel de la Fleur," where we had a most egregious waiter—a good boy, I daresay, but such a fat, slimy, oily specimen of complacency as is rarely to be seen. His French was Teutonic, and his German Gallic. Poor fellow, he could not help that, it was his nationality and "it is no sin," as Uncle Toby and Corporal Trim agreed, "to be born of a particular nation." He gave us the best of the dirty, unpleasant rooms of the hôtel, lamenting the paucity of travellers; but he told us of a great dinner given at this house the night before, by the exchanged Austrian and French officers and prisoners, to each other. I think I see him now, leaning with both hands on the back of a chair, his table-cloth over his shoulder, and his jointless, supple body rolling like an excited beer barrel, as he spoke of the toasts they had drunk to the Emperor's and each other's health, freedom, &c. He worked himself up to such a pitch, that he moved from one foot to the other, exclaiming, " Oh, it was so beautiful! so beautiful! They had fought together—they had made each other prisoners—and now they drank each other's healths! It was moving, very moving! I was touched—melted to tears!"

He used exactly the same terms in speaking of the English church-service, which used always to be performed in this hôtel, and which he had often attended.

"And shall you not have it this year?" I enquired.

"No; the Bishop of London sent us word that there were so few travellers, that he could not send us a chaplain for them this year."

I hope the Lord Bishop of London will not prosecute either the waiter of the hôtel or myself for this very innocent and unconscious libel. He probably knows nothing of the affair.

Had it been otherwise, we should have stayed for Sunday at Strasburg; as it was, we spent that day in most wretched quarters, and without a service, as we shall see.

I am afraid we did not think as much as Mrs. Hamilton Grey would have done of the history of this interesting town, and of the " great fight " of Argentoratum.*

I had always wished to visit Strasburg, so often the scene of historical and political changes; and its beautiful Minster, the wonder and the pride of successive generations.

The last day we were there Kaiser burst into my room :—

" Oh, gracious lady ! I have seen the Minster ! Oh, good God, what a beautiful, wonderful place ! There's the clock, gracious lady, with the holy Virgin and St. Joseph !

* See "The Empire, The Church;" by Mrs. Hamilton Grey.

Oh, gracious lady, there never was anything like it!"

"So I have heard," I replied. "I wish I could see it; but this is my first visit, and you see I cannot stir."

"Oh, gracious lady, no; I will carry or drag you, but you must see it—you must not go away without having seen the Minster and that clock."

I was of her opinion—as far as regarded the Minster at least—and begged to have the carriage ordered in good time the next morning, so as to be able to pause before it, and admire it, at least outside, once in my life. We did so, and I had the comfort of carrying away a distinct image of another of the works of beauty scattered over the face of this earth of ours. And whether one's stay here be long or short, it is the better for being stored with such images.

If I am ere long to tread the courts of Heaven, it will certainly matter little how many or how few of the temples of Earth I shall have seen, but while here it can only add to my store of pure and elevating thoughts, to have gazed upon the noblest monuments raised by man to his Lord's glory. Therefore, Strasburg, thy beautiful Minster shall take its place beside the cathedrals of Antwerp and Amiens, Santa Maria del Fiore, St. Peter, and San Stefan—beside Winchelsea's proud arch, Lilleshall's mouldering Abbey, and Sherborne's glorious sanctuary, and many others, relics of works of faith and zeal, that speak to man of God, to time of eternity, to suffering and sorrow of endless joy and peace. Farewell, Strasburg, if I never see thee more—Farewell, and may God's blessing, and pure teaching, come down to bless thee!

Thus we quitted this town of variance, so often conquered and re-conquered, in which ancient and modern renown meet and blend —the first and chief lodge of Freemasonry in all Germany, the most important frontier town of France, not ceded until long after Alsace itself became, by the treaty of Westphalia, a province of France. Who does not remember Dumas's description of the departure of the emissary from the bridge of Strasburg?—the emissary who was to bear to the ministry the first tidings of the signing of the treaty? I know of no parallel to it, except the silent, swift departure of Rothschild's messenger with the news of Waterloo! The one announced to Louis XIV. the addition of a gem to his crown; the other brought to the Prince of Finance tidings of new crowns for his gems.

In our day, perhaps, winged messengers are even more prompt, more ready, if not more rapid, than the electric spark, and we know it not. Strasburg has a monument to Guttemburg, to whom we owe our telegrams, and every branch of communicative knowledge. Is this saying too much? I think not. Erwin of Steinbach, and his son and daughter, Sabina, she of the grand old name and rare talents, lie buried in their truest monument, the Cathedral. In this part of the world the spire is called Flèche. I like the word, it suits one's idea of that which is pointed and directed to Heaven.

We left Strasburg early, and would gladly have visited Colmar, which has also a beautiful cathedral. And here it was that a curious record of the chances and changes of the nation's fate was lately discovered. In preparing to colour with distemper, for some fête, the refectory of the Hôtel de Ville, it was necessary to tear down the paper hangings. These were several, and had followed each other as follows:—Firstly, upon the plaster, a paper representing armour, surmounted by the Phrygian cap of the Revolution; secondly, over this a green paper, with gold bees; thirdly, a royal blue, dotted with fleurs-de-lis; fourthly, another blue paper, with the Gallic cock of 1830; fifthly, an ordinary insignificant modern paper. I suppose the present one will be "the busy, busy bee."

We should have liked to linger at Colmar, and to ramble about the Vosges mountains, at the foot of which it stands. They are not so grand and broken as many ranges—rather, in fact, of the rounded or "balloon" form—but the cloud-shadows upon them on this day supplied variety; and they are doubly interesting, as having formed the background to two pure, devoted lives, those of Oberlin and Jeanne d'Arc. It was here that the former worked, the human providence of all around him, leading all hearts to their God; and it was in this same neighbourhood that inspiration came to a quiet country maiden, and made her the far-famed, long-loved Pucelle d'Orleans. Douremy, her birth-place, stands in the collector's book of taxes charged thus:—"Néant à cause de la Pucelle"—a beautiful tribute to her.

What grand shadowy dreams must have adorned her childhood; and how, as she watched the lights and shadows playing over the Vosges, and followed with her eye their outline on the horizon—that mystic delight of children — must vague dreams of what lay for her beyond have dawned upon her soul! And in her meek, lowly life, what a consciousness of something within her, that was not herself, must have arisen, and dwelt with her!

> "She like a snow-white arum grew,
> A sheathèd weapon—when its due time came,
> Burst on the world with magic force, and showed
> A pure fair flower, with golden sword upreared,
> And single eye still looking up to God."

These mountains bounded our prospect nearly all the way to Mülhausen, the Manchester of France. Here we had to wait a little while, and were so stupid as not to get any of the fossil woods and plants with which the schistic rocks abound, and only bought some very wretched soup (hot water, and chopped onions) instead.

And here also we committed a great mistake, which I will communicate for the sake of future travellers. The railway companies are not quite on good terms here; and as they have not supplied each other, or "Bradshaw," with any exact information, we could not ascertain from his valued little work how much time would be occupied by the train from Mülhausen to Belfort, nor what would be the amount of repose enjoined at the station.

We admired the heights above La Chapelle, where the old foot-road crossed them. These heights connect the Vosges with the Jura; and here we quitted Alsace, and entered Franche-Comté. Belfort, or Béfort, a fortress of great strength, defends this pass. It was laid out by Vauban, and is still further strengthened by an entrenched camp for 30,000 men. The Savoureuse (an ill-conceived name for a clear river) waters the town. But notwithstanding all this, the station is new and wretched, and we found ourselves, at one o'clock in the day, condemned to sit one hour and a-half in a kind of shed, where eating and drinking were going on actively the whole time, and heat and noise, of course, abounded. Florence and Godfrey were so unhappy for me, that I could not be so for myself, and sat quietly in the way (for I could not get out of it), on a little rickety chair, my feet on a heap of cloaks, just where the applicants for "une choppe de bière" were passing every moment. We were amused, however, by the very business-like manner in which three men, probably well used to the place and people, asked for and obtained a very good dinner, and filled up their time most cleverly therewith—neither hurried nor agitated by the trains for and from Paris, coming and departing, nor depressed by having to wait for their own. Snatches of their conversation reached us from time to time, details, as it seemed, of the war. They mentioned Solferino, and the 300 private carriages that awaited the wounded at Milan station, to convey them to the hospitals, where the women visited and tended them. This was beautiful—true charity! One of them had been, though no soldier, present through part of the campaign. I admired their philosophy, and wished that Florence and Godfrey had been as well occupied and amused, as they might have been, had we known that this interval would occur, instead of scalding themselves, in unblissful ignorance, with that hot water at Mülhausen.

However, the longest waiting has an end; and we were at length summoned to enter the train, and passed on our way through the province with the beautiful name, Franche-Comté—now lost in the departments of the Doubs, Haute Saône, and Jura; but still recalling the trouble it has ever given to its conquerors, Burgundian, Roman, Frank, whether as the old Sequania, the capital of which was Vesontio, now Besançon, as part of the belligerent dukedom of Burgundy, when this was larger than the kingdom of France—or after its conquest by Louis XIV., in 1674, as the oft-contested Franche-Comté. It was near Besançon, then Vesontio, that Cæsar defended Ariovistus, and reddened the river with Gallic blood.

It is very remarkable how often the letters B and V have changed their characters, and indeed their parts, in human language—how frequently one has been substituted for the other—how, in Sclavonic tongues, the character B stands for the sound of our V, and how, in the Iberian dialects, they are nearly identical, and in almost all derivatives from the Latin substituted the one for the other. The history of V would be a curious work, and worthy of a clever pen.

It was at Montbeliard, the birth-place of Cuvier, that travellers used to visit the statue of that great naturalist, as at Montbard that of Buffon. Now one hurries by, only remarking the well-wooded lime-stone crags below which the river Doubs ("Doubler," critics say) winds its way. It rises in the Jura, at the foot of Mount Rixon, and flows north-east, as if to join the Rhine, but, just approaching Montbeliard, is turned aside by the ridge of mountains above La Chapelle, and flows by Clerval, with its naked rock, Montbeliard, L'Isle sur le Doubs, and Beaume-les-Dames, pretty as vignettes.

In fact, the whole valley is very lovely; it is compared by some people to the valley of the Meuse—but it reminded me of Llanberis, though less grand. These rocks are rich in fossils and stalactites, especially the Grotte d'Oselle, so named from that circumstance.

Above Beaume-les-Dames stands the ruined castle of Charles the Bold. The valley here becomes narrow and very picturesque (Roche is beautifully situated in a gorge), and then widens again before we arrive at Besançon. It was here that Cardinal Roland, afterwards Pope Alexander III., addressed to the Emperor Frederick I. the oft-repeated and memorable words, " Of whom holdest thou thine empire?" Only then the password was, " Of the Pope," as formerly "of Cæsar," and now " of the People."

The river holds on its course, and falls into

the Saône, below Dôle, thus forming a perfect water-way from the East to the South of France. A lady, whose works display on the whole much reading and information, writes to her dear friends in Paris, that on quitting the Rhône to proceed into Italy, she dropped into the river some pieces of paper, upon which she had written her last farewell to them. Her ideas of inland navigation must have been peculiar!

We drove through the noisy, miry streets, and found ourselves, at half-past five, in the very old-fashioned hôtel. It would have been wiser to avoid the town altogether; for it is low and unhealthy, stiflingly hot in summer, and, I should imagine, very cold in winter. It is still an old-fashioned town. A railway passes by it, it is true, but it is of comparatively recent date, and is not indeed finished

—not at least the branch from Dôle to Chalons, which will greatly increase the traffic. The river has hitherto been the chief means of communication—and by it the clocks and caps of the good Besançonians are exchanged for the silks, prints, and valuables of the south of France.

I was glad to see a primitive French town; and still more so, that it should be that old Vesontio; and I leaned out of my window, and watched the bourgeois and bourgeoises in their Sunday costumes. I wish I could have explored a little the habits, ideas, and customs of a town containing 41,000 inhabitants, with a flourishing trade, and a strong citadel, and yet not completely railroad-ridden. I should suppose there is no other to be seen in France, England, or Germany. It was inconvenient, however, in these days, when one is accustomed to find everything arranged so as to facilitate movement and rapidity of progress, to be in an hôtel, where, after inquiring for half-an-hour, one at length obtained warm, not hot, water for tea, and nothing else. We asked for bread, sugar, &c., but they came not. After trying the bell in the room in vain, and ringing a little hand-bell at the door, till one's arm ached, the result was the arrival, at last, of Boots, to whom the order was repeated. He disappeared, and we sat patiently, our cool water becoming cooler, waiting for the expletives, or, as some people call them, the condiments. At last, further application was had to the bell, but in vain. Godfrey called aloud in despair, and this produced a little conversing and movement in the house; the thin pale waiter arrived, with a flaring dip in his hand, and enquired what we wanted.

He was told the history of our wrongs, and that our patience was worn out. He replied, with a grin and a shrug :—

"Ah, monsieur, pardon, monsieur, mais il n'y a que moi, et je faisais une course."

He was so comic, and so good-humoured, that one could not but receive his excuse each time it was offered, which was, I believe, about twenty-five times per diem. He was waiter and chambermaid all in one—Boots the only adjunct, I believe. This was perhaps the reason that on our arrival, I, having been placed on a chair at the foot of the stairs, in full view of the passengers in the street, was left there, apparently without the slightest chance of getting any farther ; until at last Ferdinand came to the rescue, just as I, hearing a whispered discussion going on as to who should undertake the task, had determined to walk up. I much preferred it to being made a spectacle of in this queer way.

We did not then know of the paucity of attendants, but were made painfully aware of it ere we had been in the house an hour. It was quite like a scene in a comedy, and I from my couch enjoyed it much. Florence and Godfrey, at the tea-table in the old-fashioned room, turning expectant glances towards the opening door; and the tall, haggard, dirty fellow, wretched as Romeo's "Apothecary," with his eternal flaring dip, lighting up his dingy linen—and yet with a very good-humoured smile, as if he, too, saw the ridiculous position of affairs, but could only enjoy, not remedy it. No one could be angry, though it was very uncomfortable; and Godfrey at last said, when we had been waiting an immense time for the candles he had ordered, and the usual excuse had been given, "Et les bougies, faisaient-elles une course aussi?"— which made the grin explode into a laugh, the shrug become a rocking of the person, and the poor fellow, setting down the dip on the drawers, roll with amusement. I suspect it was true, and that "une course" was necessary for everything demanded.

But all this would have been nothing, had not the old inn trick of trying to detain us been resorted to. We were ready, as usual, half-an-hour before the time (half-past six) at which we were to leave the hôtel, to catch the seven o'clock train, and this was more than enough. As usual, orders for the servants and luggage to go forward yet earlier had been given, but we waited in vain for the carriage which we had ordered. Getting anxious, Florence looked out and saw the luggage only just moving off as the carriage came to the door, and Ferdinand with it, in a fever. He must have gone very rapidly; for, on our descent, he met us with the information that the train was gone!

"So we have rattled you through the rough streets to no purpose," said Florence; "at all events, let us put you down in the waiting-room to rest."

Vain hope! it was closed against all intruders, and Florence's kind face expressed great anxiety and disappointment. It was too far to go back into the town. As it was a fine day, we betook ourselves to the Café de la Gare, where we seated ourselves in the veranda, shaded with beautiful oleanders and pomegranates, and laughed heartily at ourselves for having taken so much pains to rise early and accomplish this great result. We de-

termined, however, to make the best of it—
enjoy the fine day, and forget that we had
intended to go early to Dijon. We should
rest here during the heat, and proceed at
four o'clock. I was quite happy, feeling
that it was not my fault; for we had both
been ready—coffee over and waiting, at 6.25.

I begged Godfrey to get me Dumas on Russia; but the book-stall was closed! He and
Florence took out their books; and the latter,
giving Kaiser something to alter in her cloak,
made that faithful domestic quite happy. I
sat, propped up on two chairs, on the faithful
Plank—either listening or talking, or gazing
on the hills that "stood about" Besançon,
and on the citadel, dating from the Roman
Conquest, that crowned its own rock above
the town.

Other thoughts rapidly succeeded, recalling

the scenes we had passed through; and I believe it was there and then that I formed the project of sending back to my dear friends in Russia this little memorial of the long pilgrimage that led me away from the east, from the shrine of St. Sophie. St. Sophie! how well I remember that day last year!

CHAPTER III.

Dejeûner—" Waiting "—Dôle—Our Line of March—
Dijon—Recollections—Wounded in the Train—Hôtel
du Parc—" Walter "—" M. l'Anglais "—Hôtel de l'Europe—The Old Fustiness—River Travelling—Fellow-travellers—The Rhône— Perrache—Vienne—Valence—
Montélimart— Orange—French Popes—Men of Limousin
—Avignon—Luxury of Climate—Recollections—Departure for Cette — Austrian Prisoners — Tarascon — St.
Martha—Nimes—Montpellier.

GODFREY now suggested that, in consideration of our virtuously early breakfast, and attempt at a start, we might as well recruit our exhausted frames, and accordingly we ordered a *dejeûner*, and chatted until it came.

Have we not all felt, when obliged to *wait* anywhere for hours, days, or months, so very much relieved when the worst was over — when the time, to use a very expressive phrase, had "spent itself?" I do not think one feels this in solitude—for it is easy for all to think, meditate, muse, or doze, according to their degrees of intellect and strength, when alone—so far, at least, as not to be aware of dulness; but when we congregate, our inactivity and silence are more painfully felt. The very presence of others, if we observe that they are unoccupied, or uninterested in their occupation, prevents the undisturbed enjoyment of our own pleasures; and as it is not possible in such a case to follow them out perfectly, nor even civil to attempt to do so, we unavoidably become dull together. And let it not be considered as any disparagement that we acknowledge our occasional dulness. Indeed, dear readers, we can afford to acknowledge it; and so can any one who is not hopelessly dull at all times.

Certainly, on this occasion, we had all found occupation, and were decidedly cheery and gay at our little green tables. I was much relieved at feeling better—the opium and the cigarette had fortunately subdued the neuralgia that had wearied me at Besançon. The air too was warm and delicious. I do not think the arrival of the cutlets and wine, the haricots, and the potage, was needed to raise our spirits; but they were discussed, and the bill paid, before the train came up. The bill, by-the-bye, was moderate—which is more than could be said for the hôtel charges, though they had the grace not to reckon "les courses"—surely a very touching act of consideration!

So we bade farewell to the Café de la Gare with kindly feelings, and stepped into the train to Dôle, famed for its red marbles. The branch from hence to Châlons-sur-Saône will be a very great boon to travellers on their way from Germany to the south of France. In fact, had not unfinished railways prevented our reaching Lyons in one day, we need not have stopped at Besançon; and had the Swiss railway been completed between the lakes of Geneva and Constance, we might have gone from Dresden to Bamberg and Augsburg, have seen Munich, have dropped down upon the Lake of Constance, thence making our way to Geneva and Lyons, a far more delightful journey, avoiding all this uncomfortable line of road between Dresden and Lyons. From Dôle to Dijon, and, in fact, the whole day, our course lay through a very pretty country. We were nearing the Jura, and passing into the very heart of old Burgundy—the province which retains the name having been absorbed into France, as everyone knows, by the spider, Louis XI. I was sorry not to have planned for Godfrey to see the tombs of the Dukes; but we did not enter the town, and only met a train there — a train which was bearing along its wounded soldiers, wounded not in action, but by a railway accident two stations off. Four had been killed, and many so badly hurt, that it was said they had been sent in the broken carriages to the hospital, there to be extricated; but I think this was probably a mistake, and that for "hospital" one should read "station." I find it so stated in my diary; with comments of course upon our own preservation through so many miles of railway travelling.

We were not able to get dinner in the poor old "Hôtel du Parc," at Châlons. It is shut up; but I looked at it, and at the very windows out of which Walter threw the sous to an admiring multitude of *gamins* calling him "Mons. l'Anglais," and scrambling for what was to them a rich shower, while he was delighted and amazed with the scene. He is a tall rifleman now, and will laugh when he remembers this incident of his first journey abroad.

We were sorry not to be received into our old friend the "Parc," but we found the same old sights and smiles in the Hotel de l'Europe—the same old "fustiness"—as my diary says—pervading tea, bread, water, bed, room, everything, as we observed when we were here in the autumn of 1850, and in the summer of 1851. We therefore felt the same haste to leave it, and early the next morning found the little steamboat panting away at the old landing-place, whither I was conveyed, under a splendid sunshine, in Guy Fawkes fashion, and laid up comfortably in the cabin. A river steamboat is not a bad place for observing one's fellow-passengers. In former days these river steamboats conveyed very distinguished travellers; and we met many on our former *trajet*—but now it is only the invalid, who dislikes railways—or the veteran traveller, who cannot give up the old order of things—or some one wiser perhaps than either, the visitor who thinks the fine scenery well worth the extra expenditure of time, and the cost of hôtels, who profits by them. Merchandise to Lyons is of course still conveyed by this cheaper method of transportation; and especially wine, which travels best by water.

Our travellers to-day were of all classes.

There was a lover of the picturesque, with a sketch-book—a little family of poetic travellers, a father, mother, and most engaging little child, smiling and good-humoured through all the overpowering heat of that day—one or two *local* travellers—some in charge of merchandise, some travelling economically to places on the river, and others gay and decked out in finery, going to Mâçon, or from Mâçon to Lyons, for some fête. Amongst the local travellers was one whom I strongly suspected of being a solitary remnant of an old provincial family, liking the quiet sleeping bed better than the bustling railway—the quay better than the *gare*—and the solitary meal in the cabin better than the crowded buffet. She was about fifty, rather stately in figure, and faded in face, but intelligent, and evidently accustomed to reckon by centimes.

It was amusing to watch her keen eye as she bargained for an hour's reading of a novel from an itinerant librarian, and selected warily the materials of her inexpensive but succulent repast. And she would not have it too soon, she said, though she looked longingly at our early coffee, and later *déjeûner*. "Not too soon—not till we have passed Maçon"—was her order; and a singular sun-dial I thought she had. But I quite understood her design —to make the provender *last* the day. She amused me, too, by her restlessness. Though three times the length of my person was left vacant between us, she changed her place when I was put upon the eastern side of the cabin, and went to the other sofa; and when later in the evening I found it very hot, and transported myself to the other side, she again moved, as if we could not remain together.

At length, however, she returned, and fairly took up her position on the east side. I am sure she thought me a great bore, for remaining all day in the cabin, though she did the same herself.

Our other travellers were an aunt and niece, going to Mâcon; and quite far enough, too, they were so fidgety—I am sure that they had no organ of repose.

At Lyons we discovered that no boat would go the next day; and if we were to have no river scenery one out of the two days we had devoted to it, I could have given up the lazy old Saône, despite the remnant of "*vieille noblesse,*" the dame of gentle blood and hard usage, whom we had met on its bosom, and who interested us by her history-telling face, rather than have lost the Rhône, so much fuller of beauty and memories of the past.

For what do we see of the former? What leisure have we to enjoy the latter from a railway? I did not, indeed, know before that "Perrache," the southern suburb of Lyons, from which we start, is so named from the architect, Perrache, who rescued from the streams of "Rhodanus and Arar" the tongue of land on which it stands. Thus much information one might obtain, but where the glorious views surrounding Vienne, rich in grape-covered hills, pouring out its busy little river Gère? "Opulenta Vienna!" I should suppose that name meant something, as it has been given to at least one river, and two important towns. Perhaps it means "Come!" If so, the call has been obeyed—for in ancient times riches and refinement came to the banks of the Rhône; in later, to the banks of the Danube.

In this country of the Rhône, the rocks are rich in castles and legends—the towns in Roman and Burgundian recollections; Vienne tells us of early Christians, the first Burgundian kingdom, and the Dauphins. And here, too, one thinks of Jacques Molay and his companions—for here sat the council that condemned them and their order.

Now, these fine old names, Gaul, Burgundy, Dauphiné, are merged into the meaningless " Isère " and " Drome "—probably more convenient.

There is much to visit, could one but stay and enjoy it, at Valence; but we were obliged to hurry on, and had no very agreeable recollections of this town—therefore we proposed resting at Avignon; but I believe we were wrong. The Rhône is cramped and confined at Montelimart, but expands beyond it; and one sees at intervals the snowy peaks of the distant Alps, and sweeps down upon Viviers and Pont St. Esprit, and all the guide-book beauties so often described. One ought, in travelling for pleasure, to rest at Orange, rich in Roman remains, and more easily reached from the railway than from the river, as it is three miles inland. The exiled Popes who reigned at Avignon were seven in number—of whom three, and amongst them Gregory XI., who returned to Rome in 1376—were men of Limousin, " eaters of chestnut bread ! " *

We intended to spend the 4th, Godfrey's birthday, at Avignon, and to rest there. I proposed to him and Florence a day at Vaucluse; but they would not hear of leaving me for so long. Here we were, then, arrived at Avignon. Had we come by boat, we must

* Chestnut food is said to make the wits dull.

have waited at Lyons, where, though very comfortable at the " Univers," we did not wish to stay; and should have been only at Valence a day later—no chance of reaching Toulouse for Sunday, and the Eaux-Bonnes season fast waning.

So we had dashed down to Avignon, there to rest. I regretted the Rhône scenery for Godfrey, who had never seen it; but I believe no one could have stayed upon deck in this blazing sunshine. We had written to the Hôtel des Princes, ascertaining from "Bradshaw" that our old friend, Mme. Pierron, had shut up the Hôtel de l'Europe, and retired to private life. It was, however, the Hôtel des Princes that was closed, and we made our way to Mme. Pierron's, whose house, so well remembered and so much liked, was still open and prosperous. She welcomed us most cordially, and we found ourselves in high favour, especially on promising to write to " Bradshaw," and set the error right. More and larger rooms than we required were thrown open, and every attention lavished upon us. It was very hot weather, but as we were luxuriously provided with large airy rooms, well closed from the sunshine, and with cool, delicious fruits, wines and salads, figs of the freshest golden hue, and purple grapes, it did not interfere much with our comfort.

The historical recollections of Avignon are, fortunately for our travellers in this very hot season, such as must occur to every one as he sits in his arm-chair, and smokes his faithless cigar. They need no researches, and they now require no exertion of any kind—for the solemn old Palace has been transformed into a barracks, and only part of it can be visited.

Avignon was looking just as it used to do, the most lazy, southerly, quieting, soothing of towns—just the place where one would fancy a man, wearied with the feverish, insecure life of a Roman Pontiff, retreating. There is a feeling of perennial softness about Avignon, very unedifying I daresay — but very welcome and salubrious. I am told that it is a very cold place sometimes; but I have always found the "feeling of the south" come over me at Orange, and glow delightfully at Avignon. How very different is the hottest day in the north from this bath of sunshine and soft air!

I know I ought to be very full of history, general and ecclesiastical, at Avignon; but I cannot. The luxury of living is so great here, that even intellectual pleasures are less needed than elsewhere.

I now, indeed, enter this place worn out and weary; but the effect was the same when I was younger and brighter. A haven of repose—well deserving its name, Avenio, which is, I suppose, pleasant, and not Avignon; or Vignoble, as some writers render it. Florence and Godfrey, though they would not go to Vaucluse, and though the heat was tremendous, saw Avignon; and, as everyone else has seen it, we need not describe it. One of our first inquiries on entering had been for some account of circumstances more touching and interesting than the fate of the Clements or their successors.

Here, on her way home from the sunny nest of Hyères, had ceased to beat a gentle heart; here was the wife taken from the husband, the mother from the children. But here the weariness and the pain ceased—here the earthly home was exchanged for the heavenly—the human for divine love and sympathy.

It was the second of five successive blows on one devoted household—a house where brightly burned the altar-fires, ministered unto by even the youngest hands.

Godfrey and Florence visited the hallowed grave. 1 would not do so; but read those beautiful lines that apply so well to this tale of bereavement—Keble's "Wednesday before Easter."

We had decided on leaving Avignon on the 5th August, by the eleven o'clock train, and reaching Cette early in the afternoon; but while my dear companions were out, taking their evening stroll, I concocted a scheme, which I modestly laid before them on their return, of getting to Montpellier by an early train, spending the heat of the day there, and proceeding in the evening to Cette. This, which was perfectly feasible, struck them as a very luxurious arrangement. My original plan, indeed, had been to start at five in the morning, reach Cette at ten, rest till five, and go on again to Toulouse the same night. And this I would advise any one else to do, for Cette is so unwholesome at this time of the year, that it is a great point to avoid sleeping there. It is hot and low, and the marshes that extend for miles around it give birth to numerous ills; miasma, malaria, and mosquitoes being their principal products. The railroad is carried upon quays across these marshes, for an immense distance, and cannot even then descend quite to the town. This last rumble is performed in a diligence, which adds in no small degree to the fatigue. A very ingenious and enterprising chemist has recently established extensive works here, by which he evolves from these salt marshes every variety of animal, vegetable, and mineral salts. He will probably make a large fortune, and throw new light on this interesting branch of natural philosophy and experimental chemistry. We were not aware of the inexpediency of sleeping in the midst of these *salines*, and therefore my guardians seemed much more prudent than I, to divide our journey into two parts. And I found reason not to regret it; for had we gone on the same day we should have missed a rencontre which gave us much pleasure.

Early the next morning we were aroused from our slumbers by an over-zealous courier, who, I suppose, remembering our Besançon disasters, called us at four, to be ready for the seven o'clock train, much to Florence's disgust, who could not bear her malade to be roused up at so unnecessarily early an hour. However, it was no trouble to the malade herself—in fact, she was rather pleased with the achievement; and we all started in high good-humour for Montpellier, where we were to pass the midday hours.

We arrived at the station before the waiting-rooms were all swept out, and thus found ourselves in a large one already pretty well occupied with soldiers. They were Austrians—exchanged prisoners of course, and wounded or ill. Almost all of them were thin, worn, and jaded looking. We felt much pity for them; one in particular appeared to be suffering much, and to be hardly able to travel, though it was to Marseille, *en route* to his own land. He looked up suddenly, and met our eyes; the expression which passed over his face, as he smiled sadly and bowed in acknowledgment of the compassion he had excited, was most beautiful. I longed to go and converse with him; but the uncertainty as to whether his language were Hungarian or German, Croat or Italian, prevented my doing so at the moment, and almost immediately after we were summoned away.

We quickly arrived at Tarascon, where I purchased more Russian tales, and also read the history of this city of the dragon, and of its rescue therefrom, according to ancient tradition, by St. Martha. I confess it is to me satisfactory that this much misinterpreted lady should have some good deeds ascribed to her, some honours paid to her—that there should be some faithful admirers of Zeal, no less than of Contemplation. The ceremony which was once celebrated in honour of her day is now discontinued; the dragon that used to figure in it now lies among the forgotten properties of a worn-out theatre (I use the word advisedly); and travellers now seldom stop at Tarascon, but branch off thence, eager, on the one hand, to reach Marseilles, its Crau and its Etang de Berre, and the blue waters of its Mediterranean—or, skirting the Camargue, to visit the Roman relics of Nîmes, and its surrounding valleys, on the other. This was now our course. We knew well the charms of southern France east of Tarascon, but were now for the first time to try the enchantments of its softer, greener western clime.

We passed Nîmes, with its beautiful amphitheatre—I was glad to have even that brief view of it, reminding me of many a walk in the Coliseum—Lunel, with its sunburnt vines; and reached Montpellier at half-past ten, glad to get in and repose till the evening, sending our servants and luggage on. It would have been very pleasant to explore Montpellier, a large and handsome town, but the exertion certainly would have been inimical to repose. Even the Jardin des Plantes established by Henri IV., with its Galactodendron, or milk tree, could not tempt us out. There is, as usual, a library, a museum, and some manufactures; but the most interesting sights to me would have been the making of verdigris out of grape juice, acting on sheets of copper—the chemical works of the Comte de Chaptal, and the Promenade de Peyrou, which, despite its stony name, must be very lovely.

Murray says, and I think one must agree with him, that the name of Montpellier, familiar to every one who has been to an English watering-place, as the type of salubrity and mildness of climate, will not in reality answer the expectations of those who anticipate either a soft air or a beautiful position. Indeed, it is difficult to understand how it came to be chosen by the physicians of the north as a retreat for consumptive patients, since nothing can be more trying to weak chests than its variable climate, its blazing sunshine, alternating with the piercingly cold blasts of the mistral. Though its sky be clear, its atmosphere is filled with dust, which must be hurtful to delicate lungs; and the glare from the chalky ground and white houses, unmodified by shade, is exceedingly painful to the eyes. I retain, nevertheless, a grateful recollection of the

Hôtel Nevet, where we passed the sultry hours of a splendid August day, in a very comfortable cool room, and which we only left in time for the eight o'clock train.

We passed Villeneuve, which has an old church dating from the eighth century, and Frontignac, whose delicious grapes and wine are well known. They say that at Cette there are manufactures of every kind of wine, the foundations of them being a Spanish wine, called Benicarlo, and a poor Bordeaux.

CHAPTER IV.

Cette—Wounded Officer—Agde—Béziers—Maguelonne—
Panama Hats—The War—Narbonne—Narbonensis—
M. Philippe—Mme. Philippe— His Adventures—Her
Adventures — Their Consolations — Madame Lawless —
Corbières—Hits—Caunes Quarries—Last sight of M. and
Mme. Philippe—Arrival at Toulouse—Raymond—Church
Service—Claims of Toulouse to interest—Impressions—
The Calas Family—Obelisk—Aspect of Streets and Houses
—The House Opposite—Apology for a Fiction.

CETTE, said to have been founded by Louis XIV., is situated on a tongue of land running between the sea and the salt lake called Etang de Thau. The town is reached by a causeway and bridge, carried across the lagune; it is now only five hours from Toulouse, and three from Perpignan. When we reached the railway station, the next afternoon, for the five o'clock express, we walked in vain up and down the platform; every place was taken, except in one carriage, which was reserved. Florence was in despair, and stood with me leaning on her hand, looking most entreatingly at the guard, who had been helping us in our search. He appealed to the one keeping watch over this carriage.

"Mais non," replied the other; "ce wagon est retenu pour un officier blessé à qui manque le pied, il faudra lui demander, on ne peut admettre personne avant son arrivée."

I listened with great interest, feeling sure that we should, at all events, *see* a hero of the campaign in Italy, even if he should prove too ill to admit us; and we accordingly soon saw him approaching on his crutches. When he was in the carriage, the case was put to him, and he immediately acceded to the request, but looked very shy when we thanked him. He had lost the left leg, just below the knee; he was young, good-looking, and very active on his crutches. We thought he was travelling alone; but no, a large dark-eyed woman followed us, and handed in a cushion for him, saying, as she did so, "Philippe, es-tu bien comme cela?" She seated herself opposite to him, and arranged him carefully. He seemed to suffer much from the heat, and was very fidgety and restless. She altered windows, blinds, and cushions with the most unvarying patience and sweetness; she seemed to have no thought but in him, and the marriage ring that adorned her large hand was evidently to her a link for—as a symbol of—eternity. I was longing to begin talking to them, and to hear all about his adventures; but he seemed to be in too suffering a state for strangers to venture so far.

We skirted along the salt marshes, till we reached Agde, near Onglous, whence steamers carry on the communication between Marseilles and the Canal du Midi. The ruined church of Maguelonne is seen on an island between the lagunes and the sea. The country here is not pretty, and is particularly dreary near Béziers, where we enter the country of the Albigenses. Here two travellers came in, stupid-looking individuals—Spanish in colour, but with none of the regal Spanish air and grace. In fact, they were more like the degenerate races settled in South America; perhaps their Panama hats gave them this air.

These hats do certainly most marvellously divest the human countenance of every atom or spark of intelligence. One of these poor men had a moving tale to tell, but he told it in a very uninteresting manner. He had been summoned to Italy, during the war, to see his poor dying mother; she was at Novara, and he had been so much delayed at Genoa, by the authorities, that he arrived too late. The officer expressed his surprise and compassion, and proposed to the other to smoke, saying, that he had ascertained that we did not object to it. They accordingly began to do so, but the whiffs came languidly, and the cigars were soon abandoned for conversation—the topic, of course, being the war. The Frenchman spoke very modestly of his own share in it, but with loyal warmth of his Emperor. He seemed to forget his own sufferings while exulting in the safety of his sovereign, and grew animated while describing the general feeling for him in the camp.

We were now approaching Narbonne, the capital of the Roman province, Narbonensis, which extended from the Rhone to the Pyrenees. Yet no buildings of that date are now to be seen here; the chief traces of its former splendour are fragments built into the town walls, and some tombs of the third and fourth centuries. There is, however, one large tower, which is supposed to date from the period of the Roman Empire. Whatever it contained, the train did not stop long enough for us to do more than refresh the body, at a buffet, which all except myself turned out to visit. Even our invalid companion, though he had regretted, when told how long we should stay, that he had dined at Cette, moved out with the rest, and I occupied my solitary half-hour with thinking of him and discussing, or trying to discuss, a peach, magnificent in appearance, but hard enough to have been built into the walls with the Roman fragments. Whether our dear officer had dined or not, he seemed much refreshed by his visit to the buffet of Narbonne. The light was quickly failing too; the communicative hours of sunset and twilight were drawing near; and it became evident that he would not be averse to a little conversation with us, now that the other travellers had left us. Madame Philippe, indeed, almost invited it, by counting aloud on her fingers the number of days they had been travelling, which quite authorized my hazarding the question, "Madame a fait un très long voyage?" to which the reply was, "Yes, from Brescia."

The conversation now flowed rapidly. He had been wounded at Solferino, he said; early in the day a shot shattered his left leg—the ambulance immediately picked him up, and conveyed him to the rear, where the leg was amputated under the influence of chloroform. He did not feel the blow that brought him to the ground. While he was speaking, the countenance of Mme. Philippe was worth observing. Of course she knew all these details by heart; but her pride, her pity, her glory, and her horror played as vividly on her face as if she heard them for the first time. He alluded to her coming to him—but that was too much for them both; she, however, quickly recovered herself, and told me eagerly of his having written to her at first, without saying how severe his wound was—the second time only confessing the truth. Poor thing! she was at

Toulouse, and set off immediately, travelling night and day to join him.

"What a journey for you!" I exclaimed.

"Ah, oui, madame," replied she; "mais j'avais encore de quoi remercier Dieu; mon malheur aurait pu être bien plus grand encore."

"Oui, oui," rejoined he; "beaucoup sont restés sur place!"

We were all silent for a minute or two before I replied, that the accounts of the carnage had been dreadful. "They could not have been exaggerated," said the officer; "when the Emperor visited the field next day, he was struck with horror—it was strewn with dead!"

His way of speaking of the whole affair interested me very much, he was so calm, so modest, in speaking of himself, so warm when he mentioned others. And his wife, her eyes constantly fixed upon him, seemed to be quite wrapped up in him. "You know," said she, turning to me, "this will not hurt his health— he might have broken a leg and been still in bed, or with his health permanently injured; whereas now"—her great dark eyes were full of tears. "Whereas now" said he, cheerfully, "I shall get very fat, they promise me."

"Well," said I, "that seems a long way off at present; and I think your cheerful disposition, and the wonderful activity you already show in using your crutches, are more satisfactory consolations in your great misfortune."

We then talked about Brescia, and how he had performed the journey, until the noise of the train over a very bad bit of road precluded further conversation. We tried to look out, but darkness had rapidly gathered over the scene, and I believe there was not much to see. The lake, drained by Madame Lawless, an Irish lady, the low chains of the Corbières hills, and the quarries of marble at Cannes, being the principal objects between Narbonne and Carcassonne. The latter is well worth a visit; but we rushed on in the darkness by Castelnaudary and Villefranche, on our way to Toulouse. Thinking that we were asleep, poor Madame Philippe allowed herself a nearer approach to, and a whispered conversation with, the idol of her admiration—who, I must say, took it all with a pretty, conscious, spoilt-child manner, very amusing to witness. I saw her at last, poor thing, go down on her knees beside him, and, after making-believe to arrange his pillows, cover his hand with kisses.

Of course I looked out into the darkness with closed eyes, for fear they should suspect that I had perceived this tenderness. It was a refreshing contrast to the last bit of domestic life that had invaded our railway carriage, and a very pretty termination to our railway-travelling; for we were now arriving at Toulouse, where we were to rest for some days, and where our fellow-travellers would find their home after a five days' journey.

Seeing, some time afterwards, in the *Constitutionnel*, that, at Biarritz, the Emperor had noticed and rewarded a young officer of Solferino who had lost his leg, I hoped it was my friend, though I think he must have been younger than our fellow-traveller.

We drove to the Hôtel de l'Europe, to which

we had written for rooms, and tried to get places in the diligence for Monday, having used up this week to the very latest of its canonical hours, by not reaching the hôtel till eleven o'clock. Our servants had preceded us, so that there was no further unpacking to be done—all was deliciously comfortable, and we were soon refreshed by some very bad tea and uneatable bread, a prelude to soft repose.

We found to our disgust, next morning, that although it was so late in the season, we had no chance of getting a coupé till Tuesday, and then not in the " Messageries Impériales," but the " Entreprise des Pyrenées," which promised to land us at Eaux-Bonnes in twenty-four hours. In the meantime we were to give ourselves up to the enjoyments and repose afforded by the city of floral games and religious wars, the scene of the Calas tragedy, and of Wellington's last victory in 1814. I had always wished to see Toulouse ever since my youthful imagination was kindled for the Raimondo of Tasso :—

> "Passati i cavalieri, in mostra viene
> La gente a piedi, ed è Raimondo avanti,
> Reggia Tolosa, e scelse infra Pirene
> E fra Garonna e l'Ocean suoi fanti,
> Son quattromila e ben armati e bene
> Istrutti, usi al disagio, e tolleranti,
> Buona è la gente, e non può da più dotta
> O da più forte guia esser condotta."

At Toulouse, the stronghold of the earliest French reformers, we had expected to find an English service; however, we were doomed to be disappointed, and Godfrey and Florence were obliged to content themselves with the "Culte du Temple," which is a little arid to Anglican minds. Toulouse stands in the midst of the great plain of Gascony and Languedoc, which begins at the very foot of the Pyrenees; and whether as the capital of the kingdom of the Visigoths; as the favourite haunt of the "Gai Sçavoir;" as sacred to Clémence Isaure and her still surviving Jeux Floraux; as the scene of the struggle of the Albigeois; as the seat of the Parliament of Toulouse; as the country of the gallant Raymonds; or as the battle-field of the last efforts of 1814, Toulouse is a place of interest.

But I was disappointed with its exterior, as we drove through it. The Place du Capitole is handsome; and the old church of St. Servain, the Cathedral, and the Salle de Consistoire, are interesting. The churches of St. Taur, La Daurade, and the Cordeliers are worth visiting, and Florence and Godfrey spent their time in exploring them.

Our hôtel in the Place de La Fayette looked

on one side into a small street. I could not
but fancy that some of the houses in it might
formerly have been the scenes of tragedies
like that of the unfortunate Calas — the
only pleasant recollection connected with
which is the star placed upon Voltaire's cor-
rugated forehead by his defence of this doomed
family.

The same name is given to the avenue leading to the Obelisk erected by the city, " Aux
Braves, morts pour la patrie, le 10 Avril 1814."
It stands on part of the position occupied
by Soult in that unnecessary battle, and af-
fords the best point of view for surveying, not
only the field, but the distant Pyrenees.

Unfortunately I could not see the Pyrenees
from my window; but I did enjoy observing the
habits and manners of the inhabitants, the variety of rank in the diviner sex being marked by

the head-gear, which varied from the dark cotton handkerchief to the neat white cap or veil, or the gorgeous head-dress for the Sunday evening walk. I saw into a good many little households, and in the quiet of these old streets heard conversations as easily as at Besançon or Breslau. In the latter place every child was making-believe to buy and sell, the true spirit of the age and place. At Besançon the children still revelled in toys and *bon-bons*—they were still children; at Toulouse they were all miniature nurses and flirts. One little house opposite to us especially attracted my attention; it was a little white house, with green shutters, and I fancied it must contain inhabitants whose history I should like to know. Why I thought so, and what were the materials collected by my enquiries, shall be told in the following story, in which I have entwined them. It is, as I must confess, the only case in which fiction has been allowed a place in this work. And a fiction founded upon slender facts it is; yet I think it is not by any means to be regarded as improperly introduced here, since I allowed myself to record my *thoughts* as well as my *progress* during this journey. I find that I have unconsciously moulded the character of Vérine upon that of a young and dear member of the group ever present to my mind; and though Sacontala is less an author than an artist, she may recognize herself in it, but I feel sure of her forgiveness.

CHAPTER V.

THE LITTLE HOUSE WITH GREEN SHUTTERS.

IT was on the very first night of our arrival at Toulouse, when all was still, and the hot night lay brooding and panting over the weary town, that I caught the low, distressful sound of the very weakest cough I ever heard. There was something so exceedingly piteous and touching in it, and it was followed by so painful a moan, that I could not rest without trying to discover whence it came; and accordingly rose and went to the window to listen. I had to do this several times before I was quite sure that it procceded from the upper room of a house nearly opposite—a white house, lower and poorer-looking than its neighbours, and decorated with green painted shutters to its irregularly placed windows. The next day I saw no one enter the house or emerge from it, except the proprietors of the small shop below, an oldish man and his oldish sister, for such was their relationship, as I afterwards learnt; for having heard during several successive nights the same distressful sounds, I was interested in the house, and obtained all the information I could about it and its inhabitants. It was not much, and the story is, after all, one of very frequent occurrence; but, as it interested me, it may interest others also.

"It's all nonsense! it's all nonsense!" said an old woman; "what has been will be, and what will be has been. Go, call your father home to dinner, Victor, and don't believe in eclipses of the sun. Do you hear, boy? —go directly!"

"Yes, grandma. Through the wood?" asked the boy, hesitatingly.

"Why not, Victor?—why not, my boy? Are you a Frenchman, and afraid?"

"No, grandma," said the boy, reddening. "Born for victory, and named for it, too, I will never disgrace my calling. Good-bye, grandma."

"But it is awfully dark!" thought he, as he moved away; "and the neighbours are all out on the low hill, I see; so, if the bears think it's night, I shall get no help. But courage, Victor!"

"Victor! Victor!" cried a little girl, running after him, "where are you going so fast?"

"To call father to dinner—grandma told me to go, Vérine."

"But it's getting so dark—the moon is going over the sun, and it will be late before you get to the middle of the wood; you will lose your way, Victor!"

"Oh no, Vérine, I shall not—there is time yet; let me go now, though the birds are going to roost."

"Oh, Victor, and the bears will think it is night too! Do not go—I am sure I shall never see you again!"

"There, there, my little Vérine, do not cry. Grandma knows best, you know. I shall be back before you can hide your red eyes. Give me one kiss, and good-bye."

"May I not come with you?"

"No, no! grandma would not like it. By what chance have you nothing to do, Vérine?"

"I have," she said, looking down, and colouring till her cheeks rivalled her capulet; "I have to pick the salad, and wash it for father's dinner; only I heard you going, and I wanted to know all about it."

Vérine was hardly persuaded out of her fears, but she said that the danger, if there were any, was increasing every moment.

Victor, however, asked Vérine who had explained to her what was going to happen. "Not grandma, I suppose?"

"Oh, no! she would not believe anything about it; old Antoine told us both yesterday, and said he was sure father and you knew all about it, but that a great many people did not, and were always frightened. Oh, do tell me, Victor!"

"Nonsense! there is no danger!" cried Victor, running off hastily; but, however bold he might seem to his sister, and constant admirer, Vérine, his own secret soul was by no means in perfect tranquillity. Besides the contingent danger of the bears, and of losing his way, he was not free from something like fear on observing the gathering darkness. He did not know "all about" an eclipse, as his sister and Antoine had supposed he did; and the few words she had said perplexed him. He had heard this expected eclipse talked of by his neighbours, and ridiculed by his grandmother; but he was too volatile and careless to have interested himself much in the matter.

His little sister was more in possession of

the real facts and real dangers; and these last passed so vividly before her mind, that the salad, when plucked, was washed with tears, long before it was washed in the stream; and she could not endure the suspense of waiting in the gathering darkness to see if he returned. She asked her grandmother to let her go to the hill-top, where every one was looking out for the eclipse.

"Oh, nonsense! nonsense!" was the reply; "yes, you may go—but what has been will be, and what will be has been. Mind you come back in ten minutes, for your father and Victor will be here—and hungry, too. Light me a candle, child. Are my eyes dim—or is it really dark?"

"It's really dark, grandma—it's the eclipse!"

"Oh, nonsense! nonsense!—what has

been will be, and what will be has been. There, there, run off, and be quickly back again!"

Vérine had not the slightest intention of disobeying—she wanted to hear some one speak who could tell her the probable duration of the darkness, and the amount of danger to her beloved brother; and so took the road towards the hill, and not that towards the wood.

On her way she met old Antoine.

"Going to see the eclipse? And where's Victor—why all alone? And why going out to see what can be seen just as well at home?" asked he, cheerily.

His little friend told him all her trouble.

"Gone to the wood!" said he; "gone to the wood!—ah, that is a pity! Your father was safe enough in the quarry, and could have dined in the surveyor's cottage there. Victor should not have gone through the wood to-day—he may lose his way!"

" Oh! the bears, Antoine!"

Antoine shook his head.

"The bears may be surprised at the darkness, but they are neither hungry nor cold, and will not break through their usual habits for a few minutes' darkness; but I really think he may lose his way. Had he a lantern?"

"No!" cried Vérine; and, a sudden thought striking her, she darted rapidly down the hill, Antoine calling to her in vain to say that he would collect the neighbours, and that he would soon follow. She reached the cottage, unhooked the lantern, and lit it; and then, armed with this ægis, she hurried away down the road to the wood, and was soon climbing the steep ascent, in the hollow of the mountain, already rough with stumps of trees, and darker than the darkening scene around.

She felt, indeed, that her brother might have lost his way; there was no perceptible path—stumps, bearing the whimsical forms of men and beasts, startled her on every side, and clustering branches obscured the view. Uneven, rocky footing made her stumble, though she knew the road well by day. Its length seemed endless, its darkness impenetrable. Her lantern lit but a very, very few metres in front of her. She pressed on, on, calling, "Victor! Victor!"—and feeling that it was well she had come, to see what had happened to him. With difficulty, and yet not very slowly, so anxious and eager was she, did she reach the quarry at length. The men were, she supposed, collected at the inspector's house; and she went there, selecting the hut superior in appearance to the rest. She knocked at the door. It was locked—there was no one there; and, feeling extremely desolate, she sat down and cried bitterly. But not long —for Vérine's was not a spirit easily inclined to despair; and though she had never in her life before ventured beyond the quarry, she did not now hesitate to penetrate farther into the still thicker recesses of the great wood that extended far up this side of the mountain, in a sort of groove or gorge, in an enormous combe.

"For," said she to herself, "the darkness cannot last very long—we shall then have some hours more daylight; and though I do not know the way, it will comfort Victor if I am with him—and Antoine will certainly send some of the neighbours to look for us."

So the brave-hearted child crossed herself,

knelt down, and prayed the prayer of all Christians, " Our Father ! "

Vérine was not alarmed about her father, for she imagined that he, and the rest of the workmen, had gone round to the Colline du Pré, as the hill was called, upon which the neighbours were assembled.

She was quite right—he had done so, and it was not necessary to pass the cottage, or to go through the wood by the path she had followed, in order to gain the Pic du Milan; in fact, the other road was rather shorter and clearer, and if Vérine had not thought of the lantern, she might have gone that way.

Old Antoine reached the Colline du Pré. It was a little low hill, so called, in an open space between two hills—the Pic du Milan (at the base of which were the quarry and the wood) and the Montagne Boisée; so that it was the best place in the neighbourhood for seeing anything in the heavens, unless one wished to be quite on a Pyrenean peak.

Antoine hastened, knowing that he should find plenty of assistance. His tale was rapidly told, and seven or eight men eagerly volunteered to help the unhappy father, who was in the crowd, in the search for his child. Among them was a young stranger, who was drinking the waters for his health; for this little village, though not one of the most renowned of the Pyrenean hot springs, had its season and its concourse too. This young fellow, who called himself Robert Martinet, was very much interested in the search. He could not do so much as the mountaineers, but he did what he could, and cordially joined in the blame passed upon the wretched ignorance of the old woman who had sent Victor on so dangerous an errand. They went armed with all that was necessary, in case the boy might have fallen into some crevice of the rocks. They reached the quarry; there was no trace of Victor; they did not seek for Vérine, not knowing that she was absent from the cottage. The father was distracted with fears, and every one had a doleful presage to recount.

"How the owls hooted over his cottage all last week!" said one.

"Yes, and so they did in the spring, when his wife was ill—and she died, you know."

"Poor Jacques!" said another; "he has had trouble enough of late."

The darkness was clearing away, and the question arose, whether they should go farther on, or higher up the mountains.

"Higher," said some. "Farther," said

others. "Both," said Robert; "let the four best climbers go up, and let the four others go on. We will shout from time to time, and let you know how we get on."

"Where shall you be, then?" said one.

"I will stay with Antoine, and watch and search round here—he cannot, I think, have gone very far."

The climbers dashed on—the walkers marched—Antoine and Robert remained alone in the darkening evening, searching with eye and pole every possible place where the boy might be. "For," said Antoine, "he may have fallen or lain down to sleep, overcome with fatigue, or with fear of the darkness, or may have tried to find his way, till he is quite tired out and stupid. What are you doing there?"

"Hold!" said Robert, "feel gently down

this deep crevice with your pole—is it not a body?"

"It is!" said Antoine; and Robert disappeared down the side, a coil of rope on his arm.

"Oh, heaven!" he exclaimed, "it's not the boy, I do believe!"

"Bring it up, whatever it is; stay, is it a bear cub?"

"No, no," said Robert; "call the others— I can hardly keep my footing; he is quite stiff, and I can't push him up! Sound the horn!"

It was well they had one; for Antoine was old, and it was all he could do to keep up the weight of the body, by holding fast the end of the rope. Robert supported himself by clinging to the bushes—he could do no more; and, in fastening the rope round the body, he had not only half dislodged it, but had nearly missed his own footing.

The horn was heard, and as quickly as possible did the four men return; but with all their speed Robert was as helpless when they reached him as the child he was come to save. Another moment, and he must have let go his hold—his arms and hands were numb with the tension, and his consciousness was so completely gone, that it was but mechanically that he still clung to the box plants. He and the child were both drawn up, and the men crowded round the father of Victor, in deep sympathy. Antoine, the nearest to him, was the first to exclaim:—

"It's not Victor!"—and he fell on the ground in a swoon. But the father looked on the pale face, and, lifting off his cap, said reverently,—

"It is *not* Victor, but it *is* Vérine—and alive, thank God!"

Then the sorrow for poor Victor broke out afresh; it had been calmed but for a moment by admiration for his devoted little sister, who had thus evidently been the first to seek him; her lantern still in her poor stiff hand, as if she had been resolved to shew him her little light while she yet breathed. Two of the men undertook to carry her, and lead poor old Antoine back; and to return with fresh supplies of food, &c., to their companions, who determined to seek the boy all night.

Night and day, night and day, but all to no purpose! Victor was not to be found, and the bitter grief and disappointment chilled his father's heart with a death pang. When quite sure his boy was lost, he wandered out to the little church-yard; and one who was hanging garlands there, heard him speak to his poor dead wife, calling upon her to forgive him for having lost the child she had left to his care. He told her, too, that their little Vérine was very ill. And then, laying his hat down on her grave, he bade her " good night!" and fell asleep. The witness of his sorrow knew that he had not slept till now, and forbore to awake him. He never awoke again!

The old woman, thus doubly bereaved, made her story known at all the hôtels, and a good purse was quickly made up—for the visitors were liberal; and one lady, Comtesse M—— P——gave her one hundred roubles. This was a great consolation to the poor old woman, but to little Vérine it was none; she took notice of nothing and of no one for many, many weeks. Quite stunned by the double sorrow, she neither spoke nor smiled, and many people said she would never get over it. Nor did she until long after all the visitors—Robert amongst them—were gone from Béta, and the snows had covered, not only the Pic du Milan, but the Col del Toro, and the Colline du Pré also. It was the severe illness of the poor old dame that at last roused the little mourner.

Gentle she had ever been, but now she was even more so—active, intelligent, and practical. The old lady recovered under her care; and, had she been as prudent as Vérine, their little hoard would have supported them for some time. But one day, Vérine being out, and the old dame alone, a new neighbour called to see her, and found her counting over her store. He suggested that she had better entrust it to his care, and he would pay her interest upon it.

The old woman thanked him, and said she would consult Antoine.

"No, no," said the other, "consult no one —why should you? Are you not as clever as Antoine?—and as well able to decide for yourself? I only thought to benefit a lone woman by making her the first offer; but never mind, I will give some one else the opportunity. Farewell!"

The foolish old woman, ashamed of her wise caution, and anxious to secure the advantage, whatever it might be, placed her treasure, five hundred francs, in his hands. She had still one hundred left, and had the good sense to demand a written acceptance, which was given to her.

When Vérine came home she had news to tell, and great news. Her cousin, Jeannette, chambermaid at one of the hôtels, had taken service with a rich French lady, and was going to live near Tarbes. This was great news to

Vérine, to whom Tarbes seemed to be almost as far off as Paris; and great news to the old woman, too, for she saw in it the commencement of brilliant fortunes for Jeannette, and hoped her Vérine would have the same happy fate when she should be old enough. Vérine did not say so, but she felt that she might do better still. She was very intelligent, and had always loved learning. Her dream was to keep a school, till she should be rich enough to offer a large reward to any one who should restore to her her long lost Victor; for she could not believe him to be dead.

When Vérine was observed to have understood anything a little beyond her years, and was asked how she had learnt it, she generally replied:—

" Antoine, and the Priest, and the schoolmaster were talking about it, and I listened, and liked it."

They were all three very fond of her; and she built her hopes, both of becoming clever enough to keep a school, and of finding Victor, upon their superior knowledge and great kindness.

These thoughts were busy in Vérine's mind now, when, on her return from school, and after hearing of Jeannette's good fortune, the old lady cheerfully informed her that she had entrusted all her money to this man.

"Which of the neighbours was it?" asked Vérine, anxiously.

"Jean Larune. I did not remember his name, however, till I saw it written down here —I thought it was Pierre Puyo."

"Pierre Puyo! I daresay it was. Oh,

grandmother, and he signs the name of Jean
Larune! Let me go and show this to Antoine directly."

There was no doubt about it: Jean Larune,
an honest, worthy fellow, had nothing to do
with the affair; and the rogue had put down
his name, only to be free himself from all responsibility, trusting that the old woman
would put by the paper without reading it.
Was it a proof of the innocency of the place,
that so weak a subterfuge should have been
attempted?

Antoine proposed to go after him directly.
"Oh, but," said he, "Pierre Puyo told me
on Sunday that he should go off to work at
Bagnères this week—they are building there;
perhaps he is already gone!"

Again Antoine's story was soon told—again
he found friends to aid in the search; for

though he of course intended to see Pierre Puyo quietly first, and not to brand him unnecessarily as a thief, he could not find him, and was obliged to make enquiries. Every one knew that Puyo was a carpenter, recently come into the village; every one knew, also, that he had spoken of going to Bagnères for work, as soon as the new buildings there should be forward enough to need his trade. It was troublesome and expensive to Antoine to leave his little village and go to Bagnères; but he would do anything for the child's sake, he said, and so started off —despite the suggestions of others, and of the child herself, that he should first acquaint the local authorities with the transaction, and get them to seek and secure the delinquent, without going himself.

But Antoine thought this would be harsh.

"Nay," said the fine old fellow, "if he hear me, I have gained my brother. I should not feel easy to denounce him untried. I should not like it myself."

"At least," said Vérine and her grandmother, "take some money with you, Antoine."

And he consented, in case he had to go farther. He might have gone much farther, for no such person was to be heard of; nor was Pierre Puyo heard of again for very long in the villages of the Pyrenees. He knew too well to return to the place where he had robbed the widow and the orphan of the provision made for them in their distress.

They must now, therefore, work in real earnest. Vérine must quit school, go to service, and, while looking out for a place, work hard by the day. They struggled on for some time thus, Vérine going out by the day, until one summer she fortunately became maid to an elderly Spanish lady, Mme. de Goxares. She quickly fell into her ways, improving very much in her appearance and manners by being always with her superiors. Vérine was very clever, and, withal, artless and gentle in manner. Her mistress grew very fond of her, and drew from her much of her little history. One evening, when she was very ill and restless, she asked Vérine to read to her a charming simple little story. In the dialogue Vérine read with so much play of voice and expression, that the lady gave her a comedy to read; and by degrees would have Vérine only to read to her whatever she wished to know in French. Vérine had never learned Spanish. She said, one day, that she wished she knew it, for then she could read the books of devotion to her good mistress. She was not long in accomplishing her wishes. The patois of her village is not unlike Spanish. One evening she surprised her mistress by taking up a Spanish book and reading it aloud. This was, however, three summers after Victor had disappeared, and Vérine was now quite thirteen—and even looked older, being very tall, slight, and rather grave-looking.

She had been nearly two years with her mistress, when her cousin, who had gone off to Tarbes, sent a long letter to the grandmother, telling her that she had heard of the shameful imposition practised upon her, and felt sure that she could not support herself upon the product of her spinning; "but," added she, "I have thought of a plan for you. My mistress's husband has received an excellent appointment in Algeria. He has sold his house here to a gentleman who has a large manufactory in Toulouse, and a great many houses, which he lets, and he wants some one to take care of them when they are unoccupied. And I thought if you could make up your mind to come and live at Tarbes, he would pay the expenses of your journey, and you would have a roof over your heads, and enough to live upon.

It was very kind, but still neither Vérine nor her grandmother quite liked it. The old lady felt too old to leave her home, and Vérine — whom she sent for — did not like to part with either her or her mistress. When she left her grandmother to think it over, and returned to her Spanish lady, she found her in a state of great agitation. The post had brought her news of her only son being ill in Paris, and begging his mother to come to him. Vérine's heart was sadly torn in two; she longed to devote herself to her mistress. But then her poor old grandmother? Well, but her grandmother was now provided for. Still she felt that, even had it not been so, she would rather have thrown herself at the feet of the lady, who was to her a very Saint Marvel of goodness and intelligence, than have given her up for the grasping and frivolous old woman, who was, after all, so dear to her heart, and had always been so kind to her. She almost wished she had no grandmother!—or that the old lady had been safe at Tarbes, for she felt that she could not now make up her mind disinterestedly, and hoped her grandmother would decide without her. She was to ask leave to come to tea the next night, and stay to write the refusal or acceptance. She knew the old woman would make a little fête of the circumstance. And now she felt that they should no longer be *one* with each other ; she had private thoughts and interests, and in her secret soul she now wished her grandmother to *go*, as much as she had before wished her to *stay*.

Have we never had similar struggles ? Or was this little Pyrenean girl alone in the self-horror with which she regarded these movements of her soul ? While these thoughts rushed through her young mind, her benefactress had surmounted her first burst of sorrow, and had arisen up, firm and strong in the resolution to bear all. The lady aroused herself, went into her little oratory, and thence emerging, began, with a quiet face, though with trembling hands, to prepare for disposal all the property she intended to leave. Vérine flew to assist her. She uttered no word of lamentation—she asked no questions; but, as she packed, the tears ran down her cheeks, and fell upon the nice white linen; and she promised herself, "Ah, well, I will wash it all out at the first hotel." Then she remembered that she was not sure of going, or of ever doing anything more for her dear mistress—and the tears fell faster still.

"Vérine," said her mistress, "go and take a place in the coupé for the five o'clock diligence—there are no more for to-night, I think."

"No, madame," said Vérine; and she hastened away. The cottage was close by, but she would not go in without asking leave.

When she took her mistress's dinner upstairs, she asked if she might go to speak to her grandmother, who wanted to consult her.

Her mistress gave her leave to do so, and sat still in her place, making no attempt to eat her dinner. Vérine paused, removed the tray, and, taking out a little soup, carried it to the poor lady, saying, very gently and kindly—

"Dear madame, you will travel faster, and be of more use to the poor monsieur, if you eat a little."

There were tears in Vérine's bright sparkling eyes when her mistress looked up, thanked her, and took the soup. Then Vérine cut a very little piece of chicken, and some tiny slices of ham, and laid some of the fresh salad over it; and this, too, was eaten. And then she took her a bottle of good Bordeaux, and poured some of it out, instead of the *vin ordinaire*; and when that also was taken, she cleared all away, and prevailed on the dear lady to lie down and try to rest.

Her mistress drew down the sweet little sunburnt face, and kissed it affectionately. Vérine's courage gave way, and she ran out of the room sobbing bitterly. She did not go to her grandmother's directly, feeling that it would be better that they should both be calmer, in order to decide aright. How much more she cared now than she had done in the morning about the decision to which she should come! Afraid of herself, the little girl went to the cross-road leading to the Pic du Milan, where there was a "station," a cross and shrine, and, kneeling before it, prayed fervently for direction. Let those who feel that their God is as near them everywhere, as He is to some before a cross and shrine, go and do likewise in every trouble and perplexity.

The little believer arose refreshed and strengthened. She went cheerfully to her grandmother's cottage, and found the old lady surrounded by a host of neighbours, and so excited by the brilliant pictures they drew of the good fortune awaiting her, that she had left off saying, "What has been will be, and what will be has been!"—and really believed that a new era of things was come upon the earth. With bright eyes and beaming countenance she was turning first to the one and then to the other, taking in all good auguries, till some one asked her whether Vérine should go also? Vérine was now among them, and listened eagerly for her grandmother's reply.

At first the old lady seemed to be quite astounded at the idea that Vérine could stay behind; and Vérine felt her cheeks glow. But Antoine was going to speak, and she hung upon his words. He said that Vérine should not go; that to take her from so good a place, and shut her up in a town, would be foolish; that she was earning more with her mistress than she could do by living at home; and that, if she went into service at Tarbes, she would see but little of her grandmother, and perhaps be much less advantageously placed there than she now was; "for," said he, "I consider Madame is almost a mother to her. "And besides," added he, " your wages for keeping the house will feed you, and give you something over, it is true, but not more than you ought to put by, so as to have a nice little sum to come back with "

This decided the old lady completely. Deaf to everything which Vérine thought it right to urge on the other side, she only allowed her to speak in order to smother all her arguments. Vérine then offered to write the letter, but a neighbour had already done it before she came in, the old lady was so much afraid of its not being in time for the mid-day post next day.

Then Vérine told her tale, and said that if her grandmother pleased she should offer to go with the lady, and, if refused, could then get a place at Tarbes, perhaps.

The little cottage was to be left in Antoine's care, to let it, live in it, or shut it up, as he liked, till quarter-day, when it was to be given up. Vérine counted out the rent from her little purse, and then ran back to her mistress. The lady was not asleep—she was looking at the glorious sunset, and the mountains, and she called Vérine to admire them with her.

Then Vérine pressed her hand, and asked her if she might go with her in the morning?

The lady said that she had not intended to take her, fearing it would break her grandmother's heart; but that it would be very pleasant to herself to have her little Vérine. Still she paused. "A long journey—a life in Paris—would all that be good for Vérine?"

Vérine told her of her grandmother's change of plans; and urged, most affectionately, how much she longed to go with her kind mistress.

And so at last it was decided. At five o'clock the next morning, Vérine and her mistress left their abode at Béta, and mounted the diligence. When they reached the first large town where there was a Telegraph-office, Madame sent to enquire if any telegram had come for her.

There was one just arrived. Poor thing! she turned as pale as death when she saw it, and could scarcely open it. But when she read it, she grew paler still!—Her son was no more!

Vérine, who just then came to the door to see if she wanted anything, ran to get a glass of water. But the poor lady was quite insensible. They lifted her out of the coupé, carried her into the hotel, and summoned the doctor. All in vain! The conductor of the diligence very kindly waited for some time; but the doctor gave it as his opinion that she would not be able to stir for several days, and must be left at the hotel.

Vérine chose a quiet room, and put her mistress to bed. The doctor gave her directions what to do. She had the luggage brought in, and made the room comfortable, and then sat by the poor lady, renewing the application of restoratives from time to time.

But she remained in the same state for many hours; and after that was very ill indeed for weeks of a nervous fever. This was Vérine's first introduction to Tarbes.

The grandmother arrived just as her lady was getting a little better, and more composed. Poor thing! the shock found her resigned, but it broke up her physical strength so completely, that she was as helpless as an infant; and greatly did both she and Vérine feel the comfort of their having been together when it had occurred.

Vérine was like a loving little daughter to her—watched by her, tended her, read to her in Spanish and in French when she could bear it—never left her, and seemed to have no other thought than that of being useful to her dear mistress.

This way of life went on for some little time, until the poor lady, having grown weaker and weaker, one day expired in Vérine's arms.

She had never altered her will—in which she bequeathed all her property to her son, begging him to pension her servants. A distant cousin now inherited the whole, and came to take possession, and perform the funeral rites. He dismissed Vérine, paying her a hundred francs beyond her wages. She then went to live with her grandmother, hoping, however, to obtain a new situation.

This was not easy, as she was not known in Tarbes, and the winter was now at hand. She took in work, or went out by the day; but these resources were no very great help to her; and the proprietor of the house in which her grandmother lived, sent word that he was coming to reside there, and should no longer require her services.

They now began to feel very lonely and wretched; and one evening, while they were sitting together, bemoaning this melancholy change in their affairs, the proprietor walked into the room, having come a little sooner than they had expected. They both started up, full of apologies—"They thought Thursday had been the day."

" No, no," said he, "no apologies. Thursday was the day, and I am come on Tuesday, but you need not go the sooner for that. And where shall you go?" said he, looking at Vérine, "and what are you doing?"

Vérine modestly told him their position and circumstances.

"Well," said he, "will you go and keep my house, and wait upon my little daughters at Toulouse? They are to stay there some time longer; and then, when they come out of town, my house will be sold, but you will have had time to find something else to do."

Vérine and her grandmother were very grateful, and much pleased with the place. They made M. Lesseps as comfortable as they could that night; and the next day his wife, and servants, and a beautiful little boy arrived. Vérine hoped her young mistresses would be as lovely; but they were at an unruly age, and had not the grace of their little brother. Vérine took a letter to them from their father, to explain her arrival, and began to make herself useful to them. Rooms were given to her and her grandmother, in the large, rambling old house, now more than half empty; and she was deputed to escort the young ladies to the lectures and services which they attended. They were very clever—one of them had won the golden violet of that year, and both gained the prizes of history and literature given in the "Cours" on these subjects. Vérine liked to hear them talk of their pursuits, and was somewhat inclined to wish that she had as much opportunity of learning. It was very pleasant, too, to attend them in their walks. The young bourgeoises were fond of the country; and though there was no great beauty near their native town, they were glad to get out into the quiet green fields and fresh air; and the little mountain girl liked to gaze southwards, and fancy she discovered in that distant line of hills her own Pic du Milan. And then she would fall into a pleasant reverie, only broken by the call of her young mistresses, when they wished to go farther, or to turn homewards. They told her of the tragedy of the Calas family —of the accursed heretics who abounded, and still abound here—of the far-famed Clémence Isaure, after whom the eldest of them was named—and of the fierce battle here fought in 1814, and gained by those horrid Englishmen. The heights of Calvinet and Sypierre were indeed often visited by them, and by some of their friends.

One day they met a cousin of theirs, an officer, who had lost his leg in the Crimea. He was descanting, with no small interest, upon the battle of Toulouse, with his companion, a young fellow, apparently in the army also, but not an officer. When the ladies approached, this young fellow rose and stood on one side. Vérine observed him attentively, and thought his face very handsome, and the most melancholy she had ever beheld.

The girls were delighted to meet their cousin, who was just returned from Nice, where he had been staying for his health, and chatted so long with him that Vérine began to think they ought to go home, and drew near to tell them so. They were deep in conversation, however, and were telling him, what she had not yet known, that their lectures were now ended, and that they were to go into the country directly. Vérine, as she stood and heard this, changed countenance, so much so that the young soldier noticed it. He was thinking only just before how bright and pretty she appeared standing there; and when he saw her turn suddenly pale, he darted forward to support her.

She thanked him, but declined his aid; he then began to converse with her, and the time passed rapidly, for he was very agreeable. It was at last the young ladies who called her. As they walked home quickly, the young ladies told Vérine to pack up all their goods the next day, for that they should go out of town in the evening; but that she and her grandmother might remain, and send off the remainder of their property when the house was sold.

Vérine thought her little mistresses rather inconsiderate not to have told her all this before; for she would require to work very hard in order to get things ready for their start.

They were to travel alone, and she was to secure their places in the diligence early the next day.

So, after packing nearly all night, she lay down for a short time, but could not sleep. Perhaps she was over-fatigued; but why did the face she had met that day haunt her so continually? He reminded her of Victor, yet was not like him. At all events, Vérine could not sleep; and when she arose early the same face still haunted her. On going to the diligence office, she met there the same individual. He was come to take a place for the young officer, who had conceived a sudden desire to visit his relations at Tarbes, and accompany his young cousins thither. She quickly took the places in the Intérieur, and returned home. The young soldier greeted her only as a yesterday's acquaintance; but his addressing her agitated her so much, that she never even enquired whether he was going to Tarbes also.

In the evening she begged her grandmother to take the young ladies to the diligence, saying, what was true enough, that she was very tired, and promising to have tea ready for her on her return.

She was left, therefore, nearly alone; there were still a few servants in the house, but they had their orders to follow early next day, and were therefore very busy.

While Vérine and her grandmother were at tea, they were surprised by a visit from Jeannette.

"I thought you were in Algeria!" they both exclaimed.

"In Algeria!" she said, laughing; "no. We went as far as Marseilles; there my master met some friends, and delayed going from week to week. At last he had a kind of intimation to go quickly, if he meant to have the office kept for him; and so he got a little frightened, and perhaps will really go now."

" And you ? "

" Well, I did not like it when it came to the point. I saw an old friend who was coming to these parts, and I left the family. They behaved very handsomely!" and she chinked the bright Napoleons in her little purse. I came to ask here if you were still at Tarbes," said she, " and they said you were here. May I stay and sleep in Vérine's bed tonight?"

" Yes, indeed," said Vérine, " since it's thanks to you we are here at all."

" Ah, but we must go soon," said the old woman, dolefully; " the house is sold."

"Well, then," said Jeannette, twisting her handkerchief a little more coquettishly round her head, "if it is sold, grandmother, you had better come and live with me. I will charge you nothing for your room, and Vérine will earn enough to support you. You see I am not forgetful of my relations. Grandmother was good to me when I was a little thing," and she kissed the old woman, who was quite overcome with surprise and gratitude.

Vérine thanked her no less warmly, but with more curiosity as to the means she possessed of effecting such noble deeds.

"Well, the fact is, I am going to be married; and we shall be well off—for besides my little bit of money, he has a very good business. The house is directly opposite a large hôtel, and he bakes for them."

"And who is *he*, Jeannette?" asked the old woman.

"M. Robert Martinet, grandmother; he is just my age, and you will like him."

We need not repeat all the grandmother's remarks, nor say how often she uttered her well-known phrase. Suffice it that the young man was very soon introduced to his new family, and that Vérine recognized in him the "new acquaintance" she had just made: she was rather silent, but in the general buzz this was not noticed. "Robert!" —when she reconsidered his name, too, it struck her that it might be—yes, this was certainly the young Toulousien who had tried to rescue Victor, and had rescued herself from imminent peril. But no one else seemed to recollect the fact, and she was led, by some feeling unaccountable to herself, not to revert to it.

He had been in the army, and was just discharged, at the earnest request of the young officer with whom Vérine had seen him at Toulouse, and Jeannette at Marseilles.

"But I thought you said that he was a baker?" said the old lady.

"Yes; his uncle is just dead, and has left him the business. It is a very good one."

It ought to be so; but loading guns, and kneading bread, were pursuits so widely different, that Vérine thought it just possible that he might be likely to succeed in the former, rather than in the latter; but she did not say so.

The old grandmother went, after the house was sold, to reside in the garret over Jeannette's room, and make herself useful. She was an upright old woman, and did not wish to be a burden on the young couple. Vérine, also, by her exertions, continued to pay quite sufficient for the old woman's lodging, as well as her board. She was very glad afterwards that she had done so; for the business did not answer very well. Jeannette and her husband liked better to go here and there than to attend to the shop; and their shopmen were not quite trustworthy. When they discovered this they tried a shopwoman, but she was decidedly dishonest.

Jeannette had now a young baby — Vérine a good situation. It would have been better if Robert had attended to his business; but his former life had given him no taste for so dull a trade; and the bakings were so often not ready, that the hôtel first, and then other customers, gave him up. This was a great blow to his poor wife; and Vérine thought she really ought to try and help her kind cousin out of her awkward position. So, though she had a very good situation, she gave it up on their first expressing a wish that she were at home to assist them; and she laboured so hard to inspect everything, and keep the accounts straight, that the little shop began to look brighter, fuller of fresh loaves, and there was a gradual increase of customers. She had a new sort of roll made, which she called Railway rolls; and they were so much liked, that she sold great quantities to the railway stall-keepers, and many to the hôtel-travellers. In short, she quite retrieved their fortunes; but she found it better for herself to keep away. Robert was beginning to annoy her with his admiration and gratitude; so she told him that his success was now in his own hands, and she hoped that he would go on and prosper.

Jeannette now attended to the shop, and left the baby to the grandmother's care. Vérine procured a situation in a banker's family, consisting of a father, mother, two sons, and a daughter—where she had not high wages, but much time at her own disposal; and she devoted her leisure time to taking in work, and writing a little, both of which added something to the small provision she was making up for the time of need. She sent her literary productions to the *Courrier du Midi*, and received some remuneration, sufficient to induce her to continue, but not to give up her needlework. She also kept up her studies; and, in short, led so active and busy a life, that if she had not been exposed to one or two very disagreeable circumstances, she would have been quite happy. These were, first, the very annoying admiration expressed for her by Robert, and the very great pain it gave to Jeannette—so that she felt compelled to give up all idea of continuing to reside with them; and secondly, her cousin's needy state, which made her often require help. Vérine, constantly longing to find her brother, and to have money enough to pay for setting on foot researches in the mountains, was yet obliged to help Jeannette.

Her first mistress, had she lived, would willingly have assisted her in her search for her brother; she had indeed sent one messenger through the mountains, but he proved not to be trustworthy, and never returned.

Time went on, and thrice already had Vérine thought that she had money enough to enable her to dispatch another messenger; and three times had Jeannette's distress touched her so, that she had emptied her savings into her lap, and begged her to take them.

At length it happened that a fourth time Vérine's earnings were given away. She wandered into the Parc, with her empty purse, and, sitting down under a tree, cried bitterly. Of course, the advocates of true sublimity will say that to regret a gift renders it valueless. But still Vérine's little cousin enjoyed her dinners not at all the less because Vérine had shed tears that she never knew of, over the sums that furnished these dinners. Vérine thought over her means of obtaining money, and resolved to

write more, and work more. A better
situation suggested itself to her; but she
did not like to leave those who had been
kind to her, and allowed her so much
liberty. "And now, too, M. Charles is going
away," she thought; "I did think he was
very troublesome, but now he is going, it is
all right again. Still, my poor Victor, I do
so long to know if you are really living!
And though it is now so many years since
I lost you, I cannot but fancy you are yet
alive! Well, I will work away; and I will
put all I get into two purses—one shall
be sacred to you, and the other to my
relations. So help me God!"

She went to a church—a very old one,
St. Sernin, and, kneeling before a side
altar, registered her vow by praying fervently. As she came out, absorbed in her

reflections and her new hopes, she did not see a poor wretched child, who asked charity of her as well as it could, and plucked her dress, to attract her attention. Vérine, on looking at the little creature, saw that it appeared to be miserably ill, trembling so that it could scarcely stand, and seemingly writhing in pain. On inquiry, she found that it was new to want, and had lost its parents. It wept bitterly on saying this, and seemed to be overcome with sorrow and suffering. Vérine, always kind-hearted, returned to the steps of the church, sat down, took the child in her arms, and soothed it. She was at a loss what to do with it, however, and decided upon taking it to the hospital, which was not very far off. She carried it thither; and, whilst waiting to have it formally received, saw, to her no small surprise, Robert coming down the passage. She would willingly have let him pass unnoticed, but he had recognized her.

"Ah, Vérine!" he exclaimed, "do come with me!—there is a poor fellow here who can only speak the Spanish patois, and I cannot make him understand me. He has been invalided from Algeria, I believe."

Robert did not explain that he was in the habit of visiting the hospitals, and consoling the poor sick soldiers and others laid up there; but Vérine guessed it, and her heart softened at the thought. Her little charge was found to be very ill of gastric fever, and was taken into the fever ward directly. The child wept at parting from her, but Vérine promised to come and see her. She then proceeded to visit the soldier. She found that he spoke Catalonian, and she knew quite enough patois and Spanish to be able to comprehend his story, which was as follows:—

He had been employed in Algeria against the Moors; and, being of French origin, had effected his exchange into a French corps. As the two armies were acting together, this was quite easy. He was wounded before Mogador.

"Are you then French?" Vérine asked. "But you do not speak French."

"No; my history is a curious one. I was quite young when I left France; and having lived in Catalonia a long time, I passed for the son of Spanish parents. But I was only their adopted child. I lost my way on the mountains at twelve years of age; and being found half-frozen by some Spanish workmen, was carried by them into their own village. I do not know where I had crossed the frontier, but they said they found me near the mouth of a cavern that no one could have come through. All I remember is having wandered a long time, being quite bewildered in a fall of snow, and thinking I was getting nearer home—till at last I made a great slip, and had a tremendous fall. I found myself, long afterwards, in a kind of ravine, and quite in the dark, supposing it was a cavern of some kind. I seemed to myself to have my head downwards, for I could see the light below me by turning a little; but yet my head appeared to be on no higher ground than my feet. I called on God to save me; reflecting that, without a miracle on His part, perish I must, I resolved to struggle forward towards the light; but I suppose I fell again, for I saw no opening; and of course the workmen could not tell anything, except where and how they found me."

"Where was it?" asked Vérine, who had listened with breathless interest.

"In the Val del Moro. I had left my home in the Val de St. Béta."

Vérine rose hastily.

"What is your name?" she asked, half sobbing.

"Victor Cambacères," he replied.

"Oh, Victor! Victor!" Vérine could say no more. She neither fainted nor wept, but knelt beside him, and bowed down her head upon his hands, in speechless gratitude.

He scarcely dared imagine her to be his sister.

"And you?" he asked, in a low voice.

"I am your little Vérine!" she said, embracing him.

Meantime Robert had gone home, and had heard of Vérine's renewed kindness. The daylight was passing rapidly away, and night was drawing on; but the newly-found brother and sister still chatted on, forgetting all but their joy in each other; until the officers of the hospital declared that, however disposed to be indulgent, they could not allow her to remain any longer. Vérine, her heart full, went home. She found every-one asking for her, and wondering at her absence. Her young lady had dressed for the opera without her help, and was just going out. She had been asked for repeatedly; and, besides, a messenger had come from her cousin's house, and one from somewhere else, for her; in short, Vérine could not have chosen a worse time for her absence, poor girl. Somewhat bewildered, she asked if she could at once see her master and mistress; and, being admitted, she begged their pardon for her transgression, and told the whole story; but told it so naïvely, and with eloquence so touchingly simple, that the little audience melted into tears. There was no need of further apology. All expressed the greatest interest in her behalf, and only wished she had earlier made known her sorrows, and allowed them to assist her. She was more overcome in relating her story, and in seeing its effect upon them, than she had yet been; and as if to help her to recover herself, some one, whom she had not yet noticed, came forward, took her by the hand, and said:—

"Vérine, I congratulate you, not only

upon this great joy, but also upon your having gained the silver eglantine for your last composition!"

Vérine started, and blushed—first, because she had not noticed M. Charles's presence; and secondly, on account of his words. *She had gained a prize, and he knew she had been trying for it!* She had even forgotten that it was to be given to-day.

All these thoughts darted through her mind with the rapidity of lightning; and she replied by thanking him modestly, and saying that she was quite surprised at obtaining a prize, and that indeed she had forgotten, in her other cares, that it was already the 3rd of May!

"But, Vérine," said he, "after all this good news, here is some less pleasant for you; your grandmother is, I am sorry to say, very ill, and has sent for you. Here is also another letter for you."

The letter was an offer of some work of a very lucrative kind. How glad she would have been of it yesterday! But now it signified less. She asked leave to go and see her grandmother, and spend the night with her, promising to return by daylight. She looked wan and worn-out, and they begged her to get some sleep before she returned.

As M. Charles led his sister downstairs to the carriage, he said, " I really think, Laure, that that girl is a true heroine. What a fine character!—how good and how simple are her ideas!"

Vérine found her grandmother very ill indeed. There had been one or two cases of cholera in the town, and hers seemed to be another. Robert and Jeannette were so dreadfully alarmed, that they clung to Vérine as to a guardian angel. She did not think so badly of the case, and sent for a better doctor than they had yet seen, who re-assured them, and who said that the pain and distress of the poor old lady might not be the consequences of that dreadful malady.

She was crooning out her old song, " What has been will be, and what will be has been," in the very face of her complaint. Vérine watched her all that night, and became sadly convinced that her end was drawing near. She begged Robert to go and say so to her employers, and ask leave for her to stay and nurse her grandmother.

But these people, so generous yesterday, were selfish now. They desired Vérine to return immediately, as they were going out of town. The news at the opera had been that several more cases had occurred, and they were taking flight.

Vérine wrote a mild, but decided, resignation of her place; mentioning, at the same time, her fears that her grandmother was actually sinking under the dreaded disease. She thought this must justify her in not returning to them, were they contagionists, or no.

The poor old lady died that day; and Robert was attacked also. He did not linger very long; but, in the meantime, the poor baby was taken. Jeannette and Vérine were thus left alone. To Vérine it was a very strange feeling—she had her own deep source of joy amid all this desolation, and she had not yet had an opportunity of communicating it to her companions. The poor old grandmother and Robert had died without knowing that the first connecting link in their history had been found.

Poor Jeannette's reason tottered under her double bereavement; and if she had not had Vérine's kind assistance and consolation, it is quite possible she might have lost it altogether; but she was very tenderly cared for in body and soul by her cousin, who brought to her an excellent priest, her own confessor, and a good Sœur de Charité, who soon won her confidence, and poured soothing balm into her sorely-wounded heart.

The shop was sold, but Jeannette kept the house—she could not bear to quit it altogether. And Vérine remained with her, and prepared a room for Victor—counting confidently upon his remaining with her when discharged and pensioned, as he was sure to be. All this came true—except his residing with her; for when she again went to visit him, and told him all the vicissitudes of her fortunes, he expressed great anxiety to recover quickly, that "he might go and fetch his wife and children from Spain."

"Wife and children!" Vérine fell from the clouds. She could not but rejoice that he had them; but still it was terrible to think that she should not have him; that after all her labours, and her painstaking in his service, he should belong to another. Her heart turned to the little child she had tended, who, after intense sufferings, was now beginning to recover. Poor Vérine! she felt sad, though her real troubles had come to an end, as she supposed; but she was not yet at the end of them.

The day her brother left her to go into Catalonia, a kind of pedlar, selling Spanish chocolate, presented himself at the door of the house, saying that he had had infinite trouble, first to find her brother, then to find her; but that, having succeeded in both, he demanded the reward of five hundred francs, promised for Vérine by her good lady. Vérine's little savings only amounted to two hundred francs, and of this she had just given one hundred and fifty francs to her brother for his journey. Jeannette, of course, had a little sum by the sale of her shop—but she could not ask her for any of that; and, besides, she did not think the claim a just one.

"Yes," the man said, "it was just; for had he not discovered her brother's dwelling?—and his wife and his children? Had not the wife mourned over his departure for Algeria, and supposed him to have died there? Had she not started herself, when she heard that he had exchanged, and come over the mountains, to find him? And had she not lost her little girl on the road, and fallen dreadfully ill herself on entering Toulouse?"

"Toulouse!" exclaimed Vérine; "oh! then, take me to her!"

It was, then, no imposition; and she gladly promised to pay the five hundred francs as soon as she had earned them. He led her to a very wretched house, where, in a miserable garret, lay a young Spanish woman and a baby. She was in great want, and apparently both ill and unhappy.

"Here," said the man, "here is the person you seek—the wife of Victor Cambacères."

Vérine embraced her tenderly. She did not, however, very much like her look.

She took the baby in her arms, asking its name.

"Victor," answered the woman; "and my poor little girl—oh, if you had seen her! My poor little Inez!"

Vérine proposed to take her to her home, and to maintain her until her brother's return. The woman seemed delighted; and she was quickly settled in the room lately occupied by Victor.

Vérine had now a heavy task to perform—herself and her brother's wife and baby to maintain, and five hundred francs to pay for the discovery. She often led the conversation to the subject of Victor; but she thought her companion was very reserved about him, and also about the lost child.

One day she determined to take her sister-in-law with her to see the little girl she had found, who, though very ill, was now likely to recover. The recognition of her as the lost child quickly followed. She declared that she should have known it anywhere, and called it Inez—her darling Inez! The little thing was too much oppressed with a kind of low fever to make response, and appeared to be more pleased to see Vérine than anyone else—for she kept a firm hold of her hand, and clung to her. Vérine's heart bounded. Was Victor's child now really before her?

It seemed very trying to have to wait so long for news of himself. But at last a letter did arrive. It stated that, after great difficulty, he had found his wife; she had certainly started to join him; but vague fears for the little girl she had left in charge of a neighbour had induced her to return, when she found that the neighbour and her child had both disappeared! This had thrown her into so deep a melancholy and horror of again leaving home, that she could not for the present attempt it. Enquiries in all the neighbouring villages had elicited an account of a pedlar's visit a short time before the disappearance of the woman.

This woman was then an impostor! Vérine's head and heart reeled at the torrent of ideas thus raised. She was quite alone, and knew not what to do. At length she thought of consulting M. Herro, her late employer, as to how she should act, in case she was sued for the five hundred francs. M. Charles surprised her by answering the letter in person. He entered carefully into all the facts, and saw the difficulty. That the woman must be got rid of, and the sick child retained, was pretty clear; but the pedlar and his 500 francs? He might claim the sum, and make out a very good case for himself, as having been deceived by the woman, and not a party to the deception. The woman might also insist that the elder child was hers. He advised her, however, to tell the woman that her fraud was discovered, and to advise her to go away quietly without making any disturbance, promising not to give her up to justice if she did so, and if she left the country directly.

"I think," said he, "that you will find this easier than committing her; for you have no proof, no witnesses to bring forward in this country, and it would be very troublesome and expensive to you to send her to your brother; besides, she has not deceived him, and you will find it difficult to prove the child not hers. Still, if you wish to bring the matter at once into the courts, I will readily undertake that my brother shall plead your cause. Adolphe will do it well, for he hates all frauds heartily. And as to the expense, my father says that you are to leave that to him."

"Oh, no!" cried Vérine, "I must, at all events, try the simple means first—I could not impose upon so much goodness."

She thanked him gratefully; and, when he had retired, waited impatiently for her sister-in-law's return from the hospital, whither she had been to see the child.

She came in, threw down her bonnet and shawl, and began gossiping and talking idly, as usual. Vérine felt less disturbed, however, by it than she often did—for she was in the meantime collecting her thoughts.

At last she said, "Will you sit down quietly and listen? I have something to ask you."

Her serious manner impressed her sister-in-law. She sat down, and looked anxiously expectant. Vérine's voice trembled a little as she began:—

" Where is the Pedlar?—do you know?"

" Oh, yes, he is in the town. Why?—are you going to give him his money? Have you five hundred francs already? I will carry them to him." And her eyes glistened greedily.

" No," said Vérine, " I could only give him a part of what he demands. But where does he live?"

The woman gave the address—Vérine took it down. She had determined to secure this before beginning the direct attack.

" Now," said she, " listen to me. You are not my brother Victor's wife—your baby is not his child, nor the little girl in the hospital yours. You have imposed upon me, and I ought to hand you over to justice, you see"— and she arose, locked the door, and put the key in her pocket. "You see that you are my prisoner, until the police arrive. However, if you tell me the truth, you can go away free into your own land with your baby; but prevaricate, and you shall be prosecuted, and no doubt severely punished, either here or in Spain; for you have done me a great wrong, and my brother also."

The woman looked at first alarmed—then sobbed, muttering, "It's all very fine—but what have I done?"

"You have stolen a child," Vérine began.

"How do you know that?" shrieked the woman; "it was left in my charge."

Vérine took down this admission.

"You passed yourself off as Victor's wife—

what was your motive? You were sure to be discovered."

The woman laughed, but made no reply.

"I can understand," said Vérine, "if you had found the person who promised the reward, because she could not know Victor's wife; but he was sure to do so."

"As if I wanted to see *him!*" was the reply.

True, thought Vérine; of course, she did not; and if he had been here she would have gone off, and her scheme would have been to lie quietly in some neighbouring village until the money arrived. I see!

While she was thus plunged in thought, the woman suddenly asked her—

"What will you give me to go away quietly?"

"Give you? The clothes I have already

given you, and leave to go unpunished, provided you quit France altogether."

"Is that all? Well, I will. Let me go to-day."

"Not to-day. I shall engage some one to see you away. You shall go to-morrow. Now, eat your supper while I write a note."

She wrote to M. Charles, telling him of the interview.

He wrote back:—"If she has not signed, don't let her go until I send some one to take charge of her, or send her back to me with the messenger."

Vérine did so; for the woman refused to sign any paper—saying her word was enough. She did not, however, refuse to go with the messenger.

She returned late at night, bringing neither message nor note from M. Charles. Her manner was quite altered, and she seemed disposed to bully Vérine, to obtain money from her; said that she had a right to part of the five hundred francs promised to the pedlar—that if she went away she should never obtain any of it.

Vérine felt sure that she had not been near M. Charles, and had, on the contrary, seen the pedlar. She spent another very anxious night; but the next morning she received a note, stating that the pedlar had been arrested, as he was trying to escape, and the matter must go to a trial now, for he had threatened to sue her for five hundred francs, and that she had better retain M. Adolphe, and commence proceedings against him.

Victor was at once sent for, and inquiries made in the village where he resided, and where his wife's identity must be well known.

The case was a very tedious one; and, during its progress, Victor, and his wife and baby, arrived, and also old Antoine from Béta. Little Inez was taken home to Vérine's house; and, notwithstanding the disagreeable circumstances in which they were involved, many pleasant days were spent in Toulouse. Vérine had to work hard to support herself and her family. The banker generously (from pure love of justice, he said) undertook the expenses of the law-suit, and made an allowance to Vérine for the little girl she had saved; and Victor received his half-pay.

M. Charles often came and conversed with them, and seemed to derive great pleasure from the good he was doing. M. Adolphe also interested himself warmly in the case;

and, when it came on for hearing, conducted it with great ability.

During the trial it appeared clear to all that the pedlar, having actually received from Vérine's grandmother the commission to seek for Victor, and the promise of five hundred francs if he found him, really and zealously undertook the search for some time, then despaired, and gave it up for nearly three years, but at length resolved to try again. In this last search he came to a village which he had not formerly seen. On making inquiry, he was told of Victor's mysterious arrival there—of his having enlisted and married—of his having gone off to the war in Morocco with his regiment—of his wife's despair, and her intention of following him thither.

Thus far the pedlar's tale, as told by his counsel, was quite true and credible; but here followed another curious part of his story.

The pedlar, leaving the village with these tidings, felt sure of gaining some reward, though not perhaps the whole. Once more, then, he turned his steps towards France. One day as he was resting in a posada, where he had arrived a day or two before, a woman accosted him, and said that she was Victor's wife —that she had not had the courage to go far; and having heard, on returning to her village, of his mission, she had followed him, thinking that no doubt Victor's sister would support her and Victor's children.

The pedlar, seeing no reason to doubt her word, and thinking that her presence would secure to him all the promised reward, had agreed to escort her. The little girl wandered away from them just at the end of their journey, which was very long; for not finding Vérine at Béta, where he had originally received his commission, they had traced her to Tarbes, and thence to Toulouse, close to which town they had lost the little girl, and where the woman had ultimately found her in the hospital.

The counsel dwelt much upon the perfectly honest character of the pedlar—only too unsuspicious of evil-dealing on the part of the woman. He maintained, therefore, that he was entitled to his five hundred francs and damages.

For the woman little could be said. Her counsel tried to prove that she had been suborned by the pedlar, for his own ends, to act the part of Victor's wife; and that, hearing that Victor's child was under her care, he had suggested the idea to her.

Victor, his wife, and the child, were all produced, with witnesses from their village, and all sworn to. Vérine swore to her brother, and so did poor old Antoine, whose joy it was most touching to witness. He spoke to the character of Victor, Vérine, and their parents. Everyone present seemed to be very much interested in the story; yet, though all felt that Vérine had been the victim of an odious deception, there were as yet no proofs of guilt or connivance on the part of the pedlar. One witness had not yet been heard—Victor's wife. She spoke in Spanish, but an interpreter was easily found. She was very pretty, and timid, and everyone felt for her in her painful position.

When her husband had left her, she said, she tried to be quiet and happy, as he had told her; but it would not do. So she left her little

girl with a widow, a neighbour, who had one
little child of her own; and, taking only her
baby, meant to go to the coast and embark.
But she was a long time getting there; and
when she arrived they told her that the war
would soon be over; besides, she dreamt that
some harm had happened to her little girl,
and she hastened back. Alas! her dream
was too true—the widow and the child
were gone — no one knew whither!
She was told, however, that a pedlar had
been seen in the village, asking all about
Victor, and saying that he was sorry not to
find him. They thought, added Victor's wife,
when cross-examined, that she wished perhaps
to marry the pedlar, as she had been a widow
nearly a year; but she herself was so shocked
at such a thought, that she never listened to
it. In fact, the loss of her little girl had

almost deprived her of her senses. She thought it was a judgment for having left the child. And here she fairly broke down, and wept bitterly.

Her neighbours attested the truth of her evidence, and said that she was as one dead for the moment. She despaired of finding the little girl. On Victor's return, she revived a little; but not fully, until sent for to Toulouse, and told that her little Vérine (Inez, as they generally called her) was there.

The further defence attempted for the woman was that she never intended to pass as Victor's wife, only as the guardian of his child, and that she meant to give an account to Vérine of her family; that Vérine herself embraced her as her sister, and accepted her as such.

But the pedlar could not stand this.

"No, no, mistress," he cried, "you know very well that I brought her to you, telling her, what I firmly believed, that you were her brother's wife. And as to being guardian of this child—fudge! You had lost one, and the other was your own. No one will believe that story!"

And no one did believe it. The woman was sentenced to a year's hard labour in France, and then to be given up to the authorities in her own country. She appeared to have a wholesome horror of the latter part of the sentence.

The pedlar could not be convicted, and was dismissed.

"Still," said Vérine's counsel, "as Vérine was not the person who promised the reward, she was not bound to pay it."

"Oh, yes! I feel that I am," was the reply.

"But he did not bring you your brother, nor any of your brother's family."

"That is true," said Vérine, thoughtfully; "for I found Inez. But perhaps he was really duped."

"Not a bit of it, believe me; you were, he was not."

"Well, but I promised—and I must keep my promises!"

"No; let him sue you, and his case will fall to the ground."

"I had rather make him a present of the five hundred francs."

"You are a noble girl!" exclaimed M. Adolphe.

The affair thus seemed to have been concluded. Vérine hoped, however, to keep Victor and his little family some time longer; but they were impatient to return to Spain.

Little Vérine was fit to travel, they said ; and her mother would be ill of home-sickness if longer kept away from Spain ; but they pressed Vérine to come with them.

"No," said she, shaking her head, "I must work for some time to come, and here I can work better than elsewhere. You know I have five hundred francs to pay," and she laughed.

"For getting back your troublesome brother," said he, laughing also. "I wish I could help you, since you are determined to pay it ; but I am quite sure that it is ridiculous to do so. Whom did he bring to you ? A false sister-in-law and nephew, whom you have supported during ten weeks at least ! "

"No, Victor, he brought me tidings of you ; and he did search for you. It was not his fault if the Government was, after all, the first to send you here, and poor Robert the first to find you out!"

"Did you ever see that pedlar before, Vérine?"

"No," she said, "I think not; and yet his voice reminded me of our old home."

"What! did you not see him when your mistress sent him after me?"

"Oh, no, Victor—I was always so sorry about that; she did it very secretly, to surprise me, and only let it out once when she was very ill, and thought she might die before he returned. She promised then to leave me enough to pay him—but she died without altering her will, you know."

"Did she tell you the name of the man she had engaged?"

"Yes—Iago Cazizus; that is also the name he gives."

"That is the name he gives, certainly; but I saw his old passport, and, for some reason or another, he at one time travelled under the name of Pierre Puyo. Of course this does not at all affect his claim—it is only a curious fact."

"Victor! that is the name of the man who stole my grandmother's money years ago, under the pretence of placing it at interest for her! What boldness, to try his hand again!"

"He very likely did not know that you were interested in it," said Victor; "for I think you said that you did not see him on either occasion; and your name did not appear, I suppose. Poor grandmother's would tell him nothing; but it is a curious chance."

"Yes," said M. Adolphe, when told of it;

"and I hope you see clearly now, Mlle. Vérine, that you owe that man nothing; you may do as you like about prosecuting him, but you have nothing to pay him."

"No," replied Vérine, "not if he is really Pierre; but let us ask Antoine if he reminds him of anyone."

"It was Antoine who suggested it," replied Victor, "and he was very much vexed at not having thought of it in time before the trial."

"It would not have affected that," said M. Adolphe, "since it was under his present name that the sum was promised. Look, I have brought you *Le Courrier du Midi* to amuse you!"

He laid the paper on the table, and pointed out a long paragraph, headed "Une Promesse." It was the story of the deception and the trial—very well written, but by whom?

Adolphe was gone. Victor followed him, in order to take leave of him, for he and his little family were to start the next day for their home.

Vérine read the paragraph aloud to her Carmen, her little sister-in-law, who made her usual comment.

"How curious! Madre di Dios!" and she rocked her little Carlos to sleep.

Vérine rose with a sigh, put aside the paper, and, taking Inez on her knees, made her repeat her first evening hymn to the Virgin, and her prayers, before laying her down on her little couch. The child clung to her, and lisped entreatingly—

"Tia Vérine, Tia Vérine,* do come too, in

* Aunt Vérine.

the morning! —I know some harm will come to you here, I know it will—come home with us!"

"God is everywhere, and I must stay here, my treasure," said Tia Vérine. She kissed the little closing eyelids, as she saw sleep steal over the fair child, whose words sounded like a warning.

She was left alone at daybreak. She had resumed her labours, and was busily occupied in restoring order to her little domain, when she was rather surprised to see Jeannette, who had been absent for some time, enter the room, looking as if she had something to say to her.

Jeanette, not much skilled in circumlocution, soon came to the point.

"I want you, my cousin, to give up this house," she said, "and come with me into the convent. I have been staying there these many weeks, and I like it much better than any other residence—it is cheaper, too."

"Well, well, Jeannette," said Vérine, laughing, "I think you may spare your arguments, for they will not induce me to give up my room here; of course you are free to go where you like, but do not ask me to move, for I should lose all my connection—all the people I write and work for; and you would not wish that?"

"Well," said Jeannette, oracularly, "it would be better than your living alone here. But perhaps you are not going to live alone? Perhaps it is true that you are going to make a rich marriage?"

"And with whom?" asked Vérine, coldly; for she saw at once that this was the real cause of her cousin's visit.

"With whom?—why, with your young lawyer, to be sure. What has been will be, and what will be has been, as poor grandmother used to say; and it is often seen that a doctor marries his patient, or a lawyer his client!"

"Silence, Jeannette, and do not talk such nonsense to me. Shall I get your room ready for you?"

"Oh, no, I shall come back here no more. I mean to throw up my share of the concern. I can live more cheaply and comfortably at the convent!"

Vérine was rather surprised at this total forgetfulness of the old love of her home, formerly so strongly expressed by Jeannette, and also at the singularity of her sudden predilection for a conventual life; but she made no objection and let her cousin depart, though she could not disguise from herself that it was very inconvenient.

She had not, however, much time for reflection. She promptly let her rooms and secured smaller ones in the same house, as her cousin would no longer share the expense, and her own family had left her. She determined upon economizing as closely as possible.

The change was hardly effected, when M. Charles called. His manner was confused; he seemed pre-occupied at first, and as if he did not exactly know what to say, or how to approach the real subject of his thoughts. However, with a manly re-assumption of his self-possession, he approached Vérine, took her hand, and said:—

"Vérine, will you be my Vérine?"

"M. Charles," replied Vérine, " are you

really thinking of what you are saying?"

"I am indeed," he replied; "and I have your brother's permission to address you."

"Indeed!" replied Vérine, "I think you are under a mistake, and that I ought not to consider your words as serious, M. Charles. Think how unequal are our positions in the world, and how often you would afterwards have reason to repent this hasty step. I do not say generous, because I am sure that at this moment you really think that I could make you happy; but indeed you would not find it so—your family must expect you to make a very different marriage."

"My family," said Charles, "have no right to expect me to seek anything but my real happiness in so important a matter; and I feel, I know, that my happiness lies in Vérine, and in Vérine alone. And must I believe that she does not care for me?—that her heart is fixed upon another?"

Vérine's eyes filled with tears—but they also flashed indignantly.

"You dare not ask that question!" she exclaimed; "and there is no need," she added, half aside; but Charles caught the words.

"There is no need!" he repeated, joyously.

"No," replied Vérine; "since I cannot be yours, there is no need to say anything further—is there? Not now—be merciful, and leave me, for I must rest, and work too."

She was extremely pale, but strove to maintain a cheerful air, and Charles took his leave—not mortified exactly, but deeply grieved, and not a little surprised at finding himself refused, when he had thought himself sure of a joyful acceptance.

He might love Vérine—he did not know her.

After his departure she remained an hour and a half insensible on the floor. She was roused by mice running over her face; and, slowly recalling her scattered senses, she rose from the floor and prayed.

This done, she looked round upon the very desolate little room, with which the visit of the mice had contributed to disgust her, and set to work steadily to improve and arrange it, despite her trembling hands and tearful eyes.

"Charles can never come here again," said she to herself; "but he *has* been here, and the place must be tolerable on that account."

Her labours over, she sat down exhausted. It would have been in vain to attempt writing or working; yet she dared not allow herself to be absorbed with her swift and busy thoughts.

Jeannette at this moment occurred to her mind, and, by some strange *dis*-connection, all her vain talk about the convent seemed to be haunting her.

"How unlike one's ideas of religious retirement," she said to herself; "these nuns make up worldly vanities—wash and iron ball-dresses—I do not like asceticism and exclusiveness; but still I think, if there is anything in a life of seclusion and conventuality, it ought not to be invaded by conventionality. They do it to gain their bread—then they might be ladies' maids, or modistes, and wear no peculiar garb. Ah me! perhaps a convent, after all, would be the best place for *me*. Not where Jeannette is, but something more like a convent. I shall never now marry; having once loved Charles, it is totally impossible that I should ever love any one whom I could marry. Poor Charles! But I am sure I did right."

She did not see him again for some days, and in the meantime she strenuously exerted herself to work, and be always occupied. It would not do—her thoughts were wandering. She found herself, pen in hand, ruminating on his visit, repeating his words—so few, so true and manly—and a very sincere sigh for republicanism arose from her usually royalist heart.

She was left undisturbed for some days, and received, in the meantime, a considerable number of francs, in small sums, by post, for which she was at a loss to account; until the post also brought her a large letter, containing a hundred francs, and a promise of further instalments. She was quite amazed, and the signature of the letter did not much assist her. It was from some one who bore a Spanish name—apparently that was all she was ever destined to learn. But there was writing in a different and less clear hand on the reverse side of the leaf; and then she discovered that the heir of her Spanish mistress, having read the account of the imposition practised upon her, had become aware that he had never paid her the five hundred francs named in his aunt's will, nor indeed had ever thought of her at all as having any claim upon him; but that, being old and childless, he proposed to make her his heir, if she would come and marry him, and cheer his few remaining years.

To this eccentric proposal there was, of course, but one reply to be made, and Vérine at once wrote it, and thanked him for the five hundred francs. The other sums were all sent anonymously; so all that Vérine could do was to write a paragraph of thanks, and send it to the *Courrier*, the paper that had so widely circulated the story of her wrongs.

The pedlar called upon her to claim his money. She replied that if he would wait, she would return directly and pay him a part of it—the whole she did not possess at present. She just looked round to see that he could steal nothing, slipped in the bolt outside the door, ran out on the little platform below her window, and closed the outside shutters, bolting them also. She then ran down to her friend Antoine. Most fortunately for her, he was not yet gone home. He summoned a gendarme to accompany him, who remained outside, while Vérine and Antoine entered.

Vérine produced her purse, counted out two hundred francs, and pushed them towards him, with a formal receipt for him to sign.

Directly she saw the writing, she exclaimed, "That is the same writing!"

"As what?" the pedlar asked, somewhat troubled.

"As a receipt you gave my grandmother, years ago, for her little fortune—I have it still!"

"Oh, have you? And may I see it?"

"Yes, Pierre Puyo—in court you shall."

The mention of his name seemed to trouble him; but he was very bold, and soon recovered himself.

"In court?—and what good would that

do? Who can swear that I wrote that—it is not even my name?"

"No," said Antoine, quietly, "it is Jean Larune's name; but he is still living, and can be produced to convict you of forgery."

An eager step was heard approaching. The gendarme challenged the new comer, and told him that no one would be allowed to enter. But the voice of M. Adolphe replied—

"I may, I suppose?" and he was allowed to enter.

Vérine had not liked to ask him to come, but was very glad to see him, nevertheless. As soon as he had collected all the facts, he turned to the prisoner, and, in a few energetic and able sentences, gave him a picture of his situation, and of his probable punishment, if tried; and told Vérine that he ought to be tried, and publicly exposed, as a forger and felonious character.

The wretched pedlar fell upon his knees, and begged for mercy, confessing all the depths of his wickedness; that he was indeed the Pierre Puyo who had defrauded the old woman of five hundred francs; that having spent that, and changed his name, he had become a pedlar. Hearing of the offer made by Vérine's mistress for the recovery of Victor, he volunteered to look for him, as it would be but little trouble, and might be great gain to him. He gave no very clear account of himself during the years that had elapsed before Victor was really heard of, but swore that when the woman came to him on the mountains, they agreed together that having Victor's child with them would greatly assist their enterprise; that when they found that the lady was dead, and Vérine gone, they still determined to try their fate. On nearing Toulouse they lost the child, and heard that Vérine had found her brother. They then had to skulk about until he was gone; but meant to have received the money, and be off before he returned, believing that he would either wait for, or in a very short time follow in pursuit of, his wife and children, and thus in either case give them time.

Adolphe and Vérine listened with extreme disgust to these details; and, when they were finished, Adolphe replied—

"Your confession is good for you. I have taken it all down; sign it, if you please, with the three names you have used."

"There!" exclaimed the pedlar; and he signed "Pierre Puyo, or Jean Larune, or Iago Cazizus."

"Now, give me your passports. My friend," said Adolphe, addressing the gendarme, "escort this man to the barracks, and give this note to the officer in command of the regiment passing to the frontier to-day. Leave him in his charge; but if he resists, take him to prison, and give in this confession."

"Stay!" cried Vérine, as they were leaving the room, "you have forgotten your money."

"I—have no claim to it," stammered forth the pedlar.

"Nevertheless, take it—and commence some honest calling with it in your own country," said Vérine; "repentance sometimes needs help."

He was quite touched, and withdrew with the money.

Adolphe contemplated Vérine with admiration.

"I think you are a little imprudent," he said, looking round her modest apartment, "and too generous," he added, with emphasis; "yet, at the same time, you are not generous enough towards my poor Charles. Do you know that he is dangerously ill? He came home in despair, and wept so violently, that the result was a fearful attack of hemorrhage from the vessels of the head and chest. He is in the greatest danger."

"Oh, Charles!" exclaimed Vérine. She could say no more; she appeared to herself the greatest monster on the face of the earth.

"He is so ill, that we have not dared to tell him of our misfortune," said Adolphe.

"Misfortune!" The word revived Vérine, as it was intended to do.

"Yes; the failure of Messrs. ——, at Madrid, our correspondents, has involved us and many others in a tremendous crash. My father is all but ruined. He has given up his place at Tarbes, put it up for sale by auction, and is in town. I was coming this morning to see you, to tell you all these sad events, and I am glad I came just at the right moment to be of use. Why did you not call me?"

He was trying to restore Vérine to her more natural self, for he was alarmed at the clay-cold look of her hands and face.

She could not answer him.

"Oh, Charles!" was all she could say.

Adolphe took her hand, saying, gently, "Do not let me seem too presuming, if I beg you not to deceive yourself and us by false delicacy. You do love Charles—do you not?"

She lifted her head, a glance of pride and indignation in her eyes ; but it was quenched in tears, and her head bowed an assent thus unwillingly forced from her.

" And you are not ashamed of it ? "

This time the proudly-raised head was not bent, nor the beaming glance lowered, which answered his question ; but a gesture of mute despair succeeded.

"Then come to him—you may save his life! His mother calls you—come!"

Vérine obeyed. The mother received her very gratefully. Long and tenderly she nursed the poor invalid, and ministered to the wants of all the family. They were obliged to dispose of a great part of their furniture, and to dismiss all their servants.

Vérine was invaluable to them. Both before and after her marriage she acted as one of themselves; and with her additional knowledge, and habits of usefulness, was of course more efficient than any of them. The daughter was soon married. She was pretty and clever, and not too proud to be married, "out of compassion," by a richer neighbour. Vérine's cheek burned to think of it for her, and Charles proudly felt that *she* could not fancy hers had been a "mariage de bienveillance," as such marriages were called at that time in that part of the world.

By degrees his father's affairs resumed their former healthy state; and Vérine's literary labours, so long a resource, became less necessary to the family as a means of their support. Charles, a partner in his father's bank, at length succeeded to the entire management.

Their good mother lived with Adolphe, a flourishing lawyer.

After some time had elapsed, the old eccentric heir of Vérine's first mistress died, and, to her surprise, left to her his fortune, and a pretty country house. Where? At Tarbes! He had come to live near her, in order occasionally to see the strange girl who could refuse such an offer. He had heard of Charles' love for her, and of her disinterested conduct after the ruin of his family. He saw the sale of the house and furniture announced, bought the house, and lived there until his death. He watched her continually, never came to see her, but he left her his property.

Vérine and Charles lived for some time happily at Tarbes with his old mother. They had no children; and Adolphe, who had been married for some time, was already a happy father. His wife was therefore more occupied than Vérine, and his house much more noisy than that of Charles. But the old lady was very extravagant, and unfortunately fond of gay equipages and good horses. Her son had the same taste, and ere long ceased to look closely into his accounts. Vérine remonstrated; but felt unable to say much, recollecting that she had no children to suffer by this imprudent expenditure, and that the money was chiefly hers.

One day, at *déjeûner*, the mother asked Charles if his new horse and his *volage* were ready.

"Yes," replied her son, gaily. "I am going to try them directly; but I must have a little more Bordeaux first."

Vérine said nothing, but she thought it

would be better to have a steady hand.

"Do, Charles, do!" cried the old lady, "and then you will go brilliantly!"

Charles needed no persuasion. He rose from table quite himself, but a little elated, perhaps. His volage had just come to the door. He had mounted this vehicle, which looked more like a horse-velocipede than anything else; and though it was as light as a child's perambulator in appearance, two spirited little greys were harnessed to it—in the Russian fashion, too, one at the side.

"Vérine," said he, "will you be so good, dear, as to look out in the library dictionary for the right term for a horse harnessed in that manner—I forget it."

She rose and left the room. Happily for her, she had not seen the vehicle, only heard it described. While she was in the library, she heard a sound of wheels running rapidly; and, flying to the window, saw—the horses dashing wildly away, the little carriage at their heels, swinging, falling over, and dashing along behind them! And, oh! what was that that was being dragged along behind? The old lady was shrieking, and trying to stop the horses; but they knocked her down, and redoubled their speed! Vérine took a short cut, and was enabled to catch them. A labourer came and assisted her; but it was all of no use, as far as poor Charles was concerned—he was quite dead!

The broken-hearted wife and the mother were carried back insensible to their beds.

Charles's remains were laid in his father's tomb, and his affairs looked into by his relatives. Poor fellow, he had made no will, and had appointed no executors. His numerous creditors pressed for payment.

Then Vérine roused herself—looked into their claims—sold her property, and paid every franc he owed.

This done, she removed, with her poor old mother-in-law, to Toulouse—back to the quiet street, and to the little house with green shutters. And here she took up once more the load of life.

Adolphe wished to help her; but he was himself now struggling under the pressure of a numerous family, and little able to bear new burdens.

Here Vérine lived, supporting by her pen her Charles's poor old mother; amusing her, and devoting all her powers to soothing the last days of her flickering life; for since the fatal day of the accident, paralysis had deprived her of all power of moving; a deep oblivion and childishness had settled upon her mind; and a cough, the signal of gradual decay, wore away her bodily strength.

Few who read the brilliant *feuilletons* that flowed from the pen of Vérine, guessed that they were written by the couch of a suffering, childish invalid—interrupted often by her feeble question or complaint; written, too, by one who had known sorrow so often and so deeply in THE LITTLE HOUSE WITH GREEN SHUTTERS!

216

CHAPTER VI.

Departure from Toulouse—Journey to Tarbes—Country—Froissart—Tarbes—Ascent—Rencontre—Pau—Ascent to Eaux-Bonnes—Arrival at Louvie—Arrival at Eaux-Bonnes — Impressions — Red Rooms—Description—The Day in Pau—Arrival of the Party—Life at Eaux-Bonnes —Fête Day—Games—Friends—Summer's Last Days—Expeditions—Russian Tea—Autumnal Weather—Removal to Pau—Conclusion.

WE left Toulouse joyously, at six o'clock, on Tuesday evening, the 9th of August. We left it joyously, for one is always glad to commence the last stage of a long and difficult enterprise; besides which, Toulouse was very hot, and its promised luxuries of fruits, etc., had not greeted us kindly; we had had very little, and found them dearer and worse than anywhere else. We carried off, however, one of its famous "pâtés de foie de canard," and installed ourselves comfortably in the coupé for a twenty-four hours' journey. There was not much room for extending the limbs, but Florence established me very nicely, and we both rejoiced that we had it to ourselves. Godfrey mounted to the banquette, and off we went, coasting for some way the banks of the Save. It was a lovely evening; that quiet reposing look that the sunbeams assume before they take their leave of us (like visitors who, having shown some warmth of temper in conversation, turn round with a bland smile to say adieu) shed its soft radiance over the richly-cultivated plains. And as our progress was due west, we had the full enjoyment of it.

The railway, open now to Aire, was then of no aid to us. When finished as far as Tarbes, it will enable one to reach the mountains in one day from Toulouse.

We passed, during the night, through Lombez and Boulogne, and were in Trie in the early morning, willing to believe that it was already Tarbes, but we had to wait a little longer for this.

We were still in the Department des Hautes Pyrenées, and looking on the rapid Baise. Tarbes is interesting to Englishmen; for here our Black Prince kept his court, we having had possession of Guienne during three hundred years. Froissart describes his visit to the Comte d'Armagnac. There was also an action at Tarbes, between the battles of Orthez and Toulouse. Tarbes is the key to communication with all parts of the Pyrenees. Our road now lay along the left bank of the Adour, but we had to change our diligence, and get into a less convenient one. We made use of the opportunity to get some breakfast, which was much needed; and we then resumed our ascending route—which, however, is not particularly interesting—to Pau. A little before we reached the town of Henri IV., the long, straight, aveı ue-like road was enlivened by the approach of a pretty little private carriage, with gay horses, smart servants, and a very pleasing air of luxury about it. It came up, and hailed the diligence, asking for a Monsieur Espagnol, who gladly obeyed the summons, and seemed to think the cool carriage a very good exchange from the hot dusty diligence, and I am afraid we were guilty of envying him. I saw him received by a very beaming pair of black eyes, and a little white hand eagerly extended. The carriage moved rapidly out of sight, and we felt refreshed by the pleasure we had witnessed.

Ere long we ourselves reached Pau, which has been so often and so well described, that I do not think I need say anything about it now, especially as we only dined there, and did not explore, knowing that we were to return to it to pass the winter.

The people of the hotel came in to ask if we would go on, and tried to persuade us to wait till next morning, It appeared that we were the only passengers for Eaux-Bonnes, but Godfrey maintained that we had a right to be landed there, according to our compact, that same evening. Florence and I were eager to arrive, and begged him to insist. The result was, that they gave us a substitute for the diligence, in a most comfortable carriage, and we rolled out of Pau, while the Parc and the chain of the Pyrenees were still visible—and beautiful they are. Jurançon, at the foot of the hill on which Pau stands, and on the Gave (the river) of Pau, is a cheerful, pleasant-looking residence, full of villas. The road immediately begins to ascend from thence. The Neiss waters the valley up which the road runs; the vines and the box-tree adorn it with verdure—which, indeed, is remarkably beautiful on all this western side of France.

We passed by Gan and Rébénacq, which are beautifully situated, especially the latter; and, after a long and toilsome ascent, we arrived at Sévignacq, situated on the top of the ridge that separates the Neiss and other tributaries of the Gave de Pau from those of the Gave d'Oloron. But now we entered into the birthplace of the latter, the Val d'Ossau, formerly rife in bears. The view in this descent is truly magnificent; but as we draw nearer and nearer to mountains, our enjoyment of them is necessarily lessened, so that it was not a very great misfortune for us that the rain and the darkness overtook us at Louvie, and prevented* us seeing anything more. The situation of Larunes is, however, very striking, and from it the Pic du Ger and the Col de Torte are beautifully seen. This is quite within a drive from Eaux-Bonnes, where we found ourselves at ten that night, our *trajet* having occupied twenty-eight hours, instead of the promised twenty-four We were housed in the Hôtel de Paris, not well, nor reasonably, but they said the place was still very full, though we were already at the 10th of August. However, early the next day Florence and Godfrey found lodgings at the Maison Tournée, where we were to pay eleven francs a day (fifteen were asked) for three rooms. It was dear, but there it ended; we were welcome to use the kitchen fire for hot water, ironing, and cooking, during the four weeks of our stay, and the charge for this was only two francs for the whole time!

Opposite to my windows there was the gay little Place des Tilleuls—the name reminded me of the Lipki, far, far away, under whose shade dwelt some noble hearts, some glorious individualities. There I knew I was kindly remembered—I knew that fond wishes and prayers for my recovery went up to that blue heaven, and the thought was soothing. The fond recollection of the wide, wide sphere of love and kindness with which God, in His infinite mercy, has surrounded all my way, gave me more courage and more zeal in the use of these Eaux-Bonnes, from which so much is expected there, than any personal interest in the matter. Besides the dear companions who had brought me all this way, there were other beloved members of my family already on their way to meet us. I earnestly hoped to be looking somewhat recovered before they arrived, and we therefore lost no time in securing an excellent doctor, who, though he rejoiced in the fearful name of "Manes" (which, I suppose, betrayed his Spanish origin), gave a most comforting view of the case, and moreover approved highly of the apartment we had chosen, which was just over his own. We therefore quietly established ourselves in these pretty "red rooms," as we always called them. And here it was that we laughed so heartily at the recollection of the pains we had taken to bring some red linen from Russia, for these rooms were full of it; and ours, when it arrived with the *roulage*, was not needed to complete their cheerful glow.

Florence and Godfrey would not undertake any mountain excursions before the rest of the party arrived. We knew this could not be for some days, not before Monday, at all events, and it was now only Thursday. But there was a plan which I eagerly seconded, of Godfrey and Florence going into Pau for service on Sunday, in the hope of meeting their kindred; and this was to me another of the "days alone" to be duly remembered. They left me at five that morning. I heard the carriage drive off, and went to the window; then read and thought till I rose, and indeed throughout the day was turning in my thoughts their progress, the meeting, their being once more in church together—then the separation and return. So that when Florence came in to me at eleven that night, and told me that they were all there, and all well and prosperous, I almost seemed to have known it, thankful as I was to hear the news confirmed.

The next day I had the happiness of receiving the dear Mother and three sisters whom I had not seen for very long; and of marking their improvement in vigour and bloom since I had left them. They were delighted to see all our treasures, and when our heavy luggage arrived we invited them all to leave their hotel one evening—Florence's birthday—and drink tea with us in the Russian fashion; warning them, however, that the tea must not be taken as a fair specimen, after its long journey—and that it was indeed far better in Russia. The table was adorned with a samovar, gold plate, lemon-forks—all Russian—and both tea and sugar were Russian. We gave each person a glass of tea with cream, or a slice of lemon, whichever they pleased. All thought the lemon a delightful improvement, and the tea better than any they had ever tasted. Russian bread we could not give them, nor the delicious "bubliki;" in fact, the only kind to be regularly found at Eaux-Bonnes is a very hard French bread, requiring real strength of jaws to eat it. I used to put it into hot water and sugar; and Florence having made a moving picture of our difficulties, supplies of all kinds of invalid's provender—sago, arrowroot, biscuits, &c.—had been brought from Pau by my kind Mother, and we at length succeeded in finding a very tolerable bread at Eaux-Bonnes, rejoicing in the name of Pain Anglais.

At Bayonne all the party learned to enjoy the chocolate breakfasts, which, with the Pain Anglais, proved an excellent preparation for a mountain ramble.

Every one knows the way of life at Eaux-Bonnes; for, excepting that the walking is not obligatory, it is very like that at any other springs of health. The place is very small and dull, and the invalids are generally very ill, and do not seem at all anxious to disguise the state of their health. Their complexions were in general yellow, partly from the waters causing a kind of feverish disarrangement of the system. The water is given in small quantities—a teaspoonful at first, in some cases diluted in goat's milk, or linden-tea. It was thought a good sign to begin, as I did, with a *quarter of a glass.* The water is warm, not hot, and tastes of sulphur and eggs; but I did not dislike it—in fact, the mountain air creates great thirst, so that any liquid is welcome.

The few invalids who walked while drinking the waters did so from 8 to 9. At ten there was a *table d'hôte* breakfast, and at five a dinner in every hotel; and between these hours every one rambled who could. One dear little faithful aid, however, came to me at eleven every morning, and, however tempting the hills might look, wrote patiently for me until one, when we were both glad of a mid-day repast. After which I was carried out in a *chaise à porteurs*, to sit on the little Place; or, remaining in my room, had visits from all my dear people. Sometimes my room would be gay with the products of the morning walk—bright heaths and gentians decorating every available spot; and my dear Mother, resting in an arm-chair near me, would listen to my adventures, and then tell me all the " experiences of life" that she had passed through since our parting at Ems. Looking, as she did so, so little altered by them— the same fresh, delicate face, lighted up by those bright loving eyes—the dainty little fingers crossed by a thread of crimson wool, which she was crocheting into comforters for her lovely little grandsons; or joining, in some occult manner, the diamond compartments of a quilt, the mysteries of which she had learned at Biarritz.

Sometimes we had some lively scenes out of doors, as the brightly-dressed Guides came down from the mountains, or on the occasion of some popular fête, as on

THE 24TH OF AUGUST.

The 24th of August is a great fête-day at Eaux-Bonnes, that is to say, they always have a fête at this time of the year, patronized by the visitors, who on this occasion subscribed 500 francs. It was really very pretty, and the day was beautiful We were sitting writing in my room when we heard a procession go by with what is here called a tamburine, which is a lyre or zithern, of six strings, struck with a stick by one hand, while the other holds the rustic mountain flageolet. This little procession was on its way to the church on the hill. I do not know whether St. Bartholomew's Day was at all chosen in honour of him who published the "Edit de Nantes," but certain it is that the clouds were propitious, for it was a bright warm day, in which the valley was a very cup of sunbeams, rather more so, I should think, than could be desired by the lively inhabitants, who had been working hard all day to amuse themselves and us. I did not trouble my bearers with my weight, and I believe every one had the same idea, and left them free to enjoy the sports.

These began with the *Jeu de Bâquet*, in front of the Hôtel de l'Europe. This game is not unlike the mediæval quintin. The aspirants for the prize are driven in a cart, under a full bucket hung upon a hole, upon which it is made to turn easily. Flat pieces of board are nailed to each side of the bucket, and descend below it; through these is bored a hole, into which the champion is to thrust his lance. If he misses, he receives the whole contents of the bucket on his devoted head and shoulders. Such shouts of laughter arose during the exhibition of this feat, that I suppose it is very difficult of accomplishment. Then followed the *Course aux Œufs*. We did not see this from these windows, but we heard the bell ring and the acclamations that hailed the victor. Godfrey thus described the game to me. Eighty eggs are placed in two rows, at intervals of about a metre, with a basket at one end. At a given signal three or four men start for a race of three kilometres in fourteen minutes, while two others are to fill the basket with the eggs without breaking them. And this is by no means the easier task of the two; for as they must place each egg singly, and begin with the nearest to the basket, they have at last a considerable way to run between each deposit. This is however so accurately known, that the race between the runners and the egg-placers is generally a very near thing indeed—to-day the former gained. This was confined to the men in costume. Then followed an exhibition for the young girls in costume. A bottle is hung on a string—the girls are blindfolded, and start at twenty yards from it, with orders to walk to it and cut it down with a pair of scissors, which of course go every way but the right; and when people had laughed enough at this a stick was given to them, which did at last succeed. This is called the *Jeu de la Bouteille*, and the *Jeu de la Pôele* is in the same style. A five-franc piece is laid upon a blackened frying-pan, hung on a string. This five franc-piece is to be caught with the teeth ; and, whether they are blindfolded or not, this is sure to be a masquerading process. After this followed a *Course en Sacs* which presented the usual features, but was not quite so amusing as in England, for the sack was only held round the waist, instead of being tied round the neck. However, it produced shouts of laughter.

Thus far the Jardin Anglais had been the chief scene of attraction; but now the maidens were to perform a *Course aux Cruches* from the Jardin to the Buvette, as they here name the Source. Godfrey called this carrying coals to Newcastle.

He came in to tell me to look out, and I was just in time to see four well-built girls move swiftly and steadily up the hill with brimming buckets of water on their heads.

One was already decidedly in advance, and she kept her advantage. We saw her come in winner; and we were amused to see four or five others, who had no chance of even a second prize, come sailing on after the four first, as if they thought the race were still to be won.

There was after this a general *pour down* to the Jardin, and the busy crowds passed away from our sight, the black hats and dresses of our Spanish and would-be Spanish waterdrinkers mingling with the bright red jackets, girdles, and capulets of the natives. The capulet is, by-the-way, something between the mantilla and the Maltese faldette, and is no doubt a relic of the Moorish yashmak, which still may be seen at Bayonne, I am told.

Nothing more appeared for some time, until, as we were looking up to the green mountain nearest to the town, we descried the white shirts of four or five men; they appeared, however, like mites climbing its rugged sides. It was interesting to observe them— at one time the second man appeared to be gaining on the first, and we all thought he would beat him; but no, the first man kept ahead, and in ten minutes from the moment of starting stood beside the umpire, who held and waved a tricolor flag on the summit, and within the prescribed twenty minutes the second also reached the goal. Poor fellows, I hope they were well rewarded for it, for it was no slight exertion to climb that hill-side in the blazing sunshine! And as we watched them mounting the glassy slopes, or clambering over the rocky prominences that make a sort of staircase on its huge flanks, we grew out of breath, and seemed to feel with them the changing exertion from the long stride that satisfactorily made use of the rocks to the short, careful footsteps needed to avoid slipping on the burnt grass. Just at the last there was a fierce bit of climbing—hand, and foot, and knee, all pressed into the service. There is a ridge of rocks there, which forms, as it were, a sort of neck to the hill, after which the ascent is a slope to the summit, during which we lost sight of them for a few minutes, and they only re-appeared when victorious. They descended into our Place, where they were received with shouts and acclamations by the quickly-increasing crowd, already forming for a dance, called in the programme, Concours de Danses Ossalaises (Saut Basque). From my chair in the window I watched them very comfortably. These dances begin with a joining of hands in a circle, and moving round to a well-marked air, something like a strathspey, but slower, and the step is not unlike that of the Scotch dances—that is the type to which it belongs. It is also accompanied by cries, and is like them, moreover, in this, that it is danced in time so true, that a deaf man might guess the measure.

At the moment they scream they make the *Saut Basque*—a violent movement by which one leg describes a sweep in the air, and coming down receives the whole weight of the body, while the other is brought forward with a jerk. This is very faintly shadowed in the Pas de Basque taught in our dancing academies, though the mechanism is the same. In the first dance—the *Danse des Guides*—the men alone took part, and they do dance beautifully. Their dress, too, is very pretty and picturesque—black, deep brown, or white gaiters and shoes, black velvet knee-breeches, white waistcoats, and short sleeves, with a brilliant scarlet jacket hanging over the shoulder, a *ceinture* of the same colour, and the brown *berret*, which is a flat stiff cap, quite round and brimless, with a scarlet loop and tassel. The hair is worn long and curling on their shoulders. The greatest dancer on this occasion was further adorned with a medal of some kind, and scarlet ribbons on his white waistcoat. He had evidently an eye for effect, and no small notion of his own merits. I observed that when they came to the single steps, which they dance in a ring, but separately, everyone kept at a respectful distance from him; and when the dance was changed without his consent he disappeared, and was seen no more. It was rather difficult to distinguish whether the " Danse des

Montagnards" was a general or specific name. I myself think the former, and that it included not only the brilliant *Danse des Guides*, with the Saut Basque, which we saw first, but also the next, a slower, sadder step, in which the women took part—and the particularly pretty one that followed.

In this last they stand alternately, a man and a woman, all in costume;—the men as already described; the women in closely-plaited dark woollen shirts, reaching to the ancle, with a short low bodice or stay over a yellow and red handkerchief—the capulet and a fold of muslin under it. They join hands, and, making two or three light steps, ending in a demi-volte, face their partners "pour balancer"; the first man, taking his partner by the waist, looks as if he wished for a *tour de valse* and could not get it, for he immediately has to resume his position, and proceed with the moving chain. After this a sort of master of the ceremonies rang a bell, and announced that the *Courses aux Anes* would take place. This was followed by the *Course aux Chevaux*, an *impromptu*, and very bad.

More dancing and a fire balloon continued the evening sports for the populace, just as the bourgeoisie began to repair to the Hôtel des Princes for a concert and ball, which was, as Kaiser informed me, "sehr elegant." I hope she did not dance, for she makes one's teeth chatter when she crosses the room.

Thus ended this long, hard-working day of amusement, during which the good humour was as uninterrupted as the sunshine. All the gay world, who had been filling the windows and lounging about to look at them, had now dispersed to recruit exhausted nature; while the actors in the scene may perhaps have gone away in detachments and returned, but appeared to be always *en evidence,* and not to think of rest, or eating or drinking; whereas in England the roast beef and plum-pudding would certainly have been neither last nor least in the attractions of the day. One little torment still survives, as a memorial of the 24th of August, in the boys' pipes that scream like miniature but incessant steam-engines through the valley.

One pleasant souvenir of Eaux-Bonnes must find a place here.

The invalids whom I saw from my windows on the little Place, walking up and down during the intervals of taking their glasses of water, were some young, some old, some gay, some grave, but all ill enough to excite compassion and sympathy. One lady, especially, and her companion, attracted my attention. The elder lady looked like an Englishwoman, the younger like a Russian. It proved that they were so; that they had also noticed me at my window; and ere long I had the pleasure of making acquaintance with them both. The English lady was to be also our neighbour at Pau; the younger, with her invalid mother, and a little sister and brother—the two children had danced the Pas des Montagnards beautifully—soon left Eaux-Bonnes for Paris, where, not knowing that the poor invalid had died soon after their arrival there, I hoped to meet them again.

And now the days were growing short

and cold; evening rambles on the hills were given up, and I begged that evening visits to me might also be discontinued. Yet tourists poured daily into Eaux-Bonnes, intent on mountain excursions—now up the Pic du Gers, now further away by Eaux-Chaudes, and Gabas, into Spain. One adventurous Englishman, a friend of ours, was indeed going to escort his sister to Panticosa, and thence to Cauterêts. They were both good mountaineers, and clever, enterprising people; but the weather, so uncertain in the mountains at this season, made it a very trying expedition, and they dissuaded our party from doing more than a visit to Gabas, which they accomplished on a glorious day early in September. The last glorious day we had; for the hills were soon snow-sprinkled — the cold increased, and the mountain air became more difficult to breathe than ever. My dear Mother drove into Pau, and secured a charming house, in full view of the Pyrenees, to which we had become attached by our residence among them. I must not, however, attempt to say anything in detail, either of them or of Eaux-Bonnes; for what can one see while only driving to Laruns, or carried to the Promenade Horizontale, or the Baths, in a *Chaise à Porteurs?* Beautiful effects, suddenly changing, of light, and shade, and colour, on glorious mountains, for the nourishing of my own fancy; but nothing that could guide or interest other invalids there.

Cheered by the arrival of another brother, we passed languidly through the first half of September; but now the higher points were getting hoar-headed; the winds that swept down from them were chilling; the cold became—first pinching, then annoying, then severe; and we all thought longingly of the pretty house awaiting us at Pau, and of the softer air and longer hours of sunshine we should find farther from the mountains.

I was truly thankful when G—— had seen enough of Eaux-Bonnes, and meditated a trip into Spain, with Godfrey, from Pau. Everyone was therefore ready to start; and on the 20th of September we followed our dear party, who had gone two days before to prepare for us.

The story of my wanderings is perhaps not yet ended. Contrary to my expectations, I performed this journey *on a plank*. But the history of the original plank is now ended. It has rejoined its fellow, and contains my books, decorating the charming room that loving hands have prepared for me; and reminding me, as so many other objects do, of the land they and I come from—Russia. I lie on my sofa, looking at the lovely Pyrenees reflected in a large mirror. That mirror reflects also the many treasures around me — the alabaster, the malachite, the beautiful images, and gold lamp above my head—the goblet and service of Caucasian work, the coral rosary, and the turquoise ring on my hand—all, all speak, fondly speak, of happy days gone by—and of more than kind love and friendship, prized, words fail to express how fondly and how faithfully.

Thus surrounded, I unwillingly close my little work, and bid it adieu! Adieu also to you, kind, patient reader, who have borne with me so long! And adieu—oh, let it not be for ever!—to those dear, dear friends, those beautiful natures, who have made the words "Russia" and "Russian" dear to me for evermore! Heaven bless you, dearly beloved, and be with you all! Amen.

 Maison Faisan,
  Pau, *October*, 1859.

VERSES AND TRANSLATIONS

FROM

THE RUSSIAN.

VERSES AND TRANSLATIONS.

THE PINE.

In the rugged North there stands alone,
   On naked peak, the pine,
And dreams and waves as unseen winds
   His snow-stoled form incline.

He dreams how afar in the distant land,
   Whence the morning sunshine brings,
Sad and alone 'mid the burning plain,
   One lovely Palm-tree springs.

                      LERMONTOV.
                          (VIOLA, TR.)

CLOUDS.

Clouds of Heaven, eternal travellers,
   Pearl-threaded o'er the azure plain,
Say, are ye, like me, exiled wanderers,
   The dear North longing to regain?

Oh! what pursues you?—Sentence dread?
   Secret manœuvre? or open hate?
Or the venomed dart by Envy sped?
   Or the "friendly counsel," all too late?

Oh, no! far above all cares are ye,
   Passion and grief to you are strange,
Eternally cold, eternally free,
   Nought is exile, nought home, in your
      ceaseless range.

                        Lermontov.
                            (Viola, Tr.)

THE ANGEL.

'Neath the midnight sky an angel winged his way,
   And sang a low sweet strain ;   [lay,
And moon, and stars, and clouds, attentive to his
   Came near—a rev'rent train.

Of the bright and innocent spirits he sang
   In Eden's bowers that stray ;
Of the Infinite Glorious God—and there rang
   No echo false in his lay.

A young soul lay folded in his fond embrace,
   For this earth of grief and tears ;
And his song, like a wordless melody, trace
   Left in that young soul's ears.

Long lingered she on this earth, and she pined
   With wistful longings vain,   [find
And in none of earth's loveliest songs could she
   The charm of that heavenly strain.

                              Lermontov.
                              (Viola, Tr.)

A SAIL.

WHITE, on the dark-blue ocean mist,
    A lonely sail appears;
What seeks she here on this distant shore?
    Or what in her own land fears?

The waves dash round her, the winds call loud,
    The tall mast bends and cries;
Alas! no happiness here doth she find,
    Nor yet from happiness flies.

Behind her there glistens a wake of light,
    The sunbeams gild her crest,
Oh! why will she tempests wild demand,
    As if storms alone brought rest?

                    LERMONTOV.
                      (VIOLA, TR.)

A WISH.

In sculptured tomb I would not rest,
  With vain magnificence around,
Shut out from those I love the best,
  And trusted to the death-cold ground.

Nor would I be embalmed, and lie
  A check on all their heedless glee,
Of life a ghastly mockery,
  In annual spectacle to be.

Nor would I choose (tho' that were gain)
  'Neath the old yew beside the stream,
That spot, when shadows of our fane
  Fall 'thwart the moon-beams' silver gleam.

There, it is true, the thought of me
  Oft in each gentle heart might rise,
And still, whene'er they came to pray,
  Win a soft glance from those dear eyes.

I would not in their garden lie,
    Though nearer to their daily life,
Though there, with sweetest minstrelsy,
    From those dear lips, the air be rife.

No! let me rather shrink away,
    Till by the spicy flame consumed;
Then let a hand belovèd lay
    Mine ashes in a fold perfumed.

And this the warm and beating heart,
    For ever on its pulses wear;
So might I still my loving part
    In all its joys and sorrows bear!

                        (VIOLA, TR.)

THE ROCK AND THE WAVE.

SEEST thou that proud and beauteous rock,
    The sunshine gilding her fair head ;
While at her feet, with sudden shock,
    The ocean calls upon its dead ?

Come, wander here next century,
    That rock shall hold its own no more ;
The sea shall boast its gluttony,
    And feast upon a crumbled shore.

Ah me !—it doth remind of one
    Whose tale too often, sadly true,
Proves but how weak is pride alone,
    How strong—a fervour ever new !

Like some fair rock, in radiance grave,
    The sky and sea with smiles did greet;
He, like the restless, longing wave,
    Returned for ever to her feet.

But never could he reach her thought,
    Nor gain the slightest smile from her;
While sunshine all around her brought
    The wooing of the summer air.

But once when summer southwards flew,
    Once when the sky was overcast,
He did his daily vow renew—
    She leapt into his arms at last.

VIOLA.

THE THORNE-STAFFE.

"Thou bent and stricken, wearie Thorne,
The blasts and bolts that thou hast borne
Have overcome thy glance of pride,
Yea, reft thee blossoms silver-eyed!"

Thus did I sing thee, wearie Thorne,
And counte the tempests thou hadst borne;
Finding therein a likeness strange,
To one I knowe—one life of change.

Yet wert thou wreathèd erst so gaye,
They claimed thee for the bonnie Maye;
And bid thee be that month's owne tree—
Alas! how all is changed for thee!

So was it with that childe of Maye,
Whose life is haunting me to-daye;
Like thine it promised flower and sheen,
But bent and faded now 'tis seen.

Yet from thy knotty boughs they take
A fragmente, relique-staff to make,—
To aide the Pilgrim to the shrine,
Or to the grave, poor Thorne—be thine!

A Staffe some feeble foote to aide,
To holy roode, or saintely shade!—
Oh, mighte such be that childe of Maye,
Whose life is haunting me to-daye!

VIOLA.

Sept. 1, 1859.

THE DOVE.

" NAY, child, harm not the gentle dove,
    For man 'tis no fit food—
The Image of the Mind above,
    The Angel of the Flood!"

" But, mother, we have nought in store,
    No cashia, quass, nor meal;
The stove, alas, we heat no more,
    How cold the walls now feel!

"You will not yet th' intendant seek,
    Nor help from our good lord;"
"True, child, and thou art pale and weak,
    Yet list the sacred Word.

" When first the earth 'neath waters lay,
    The Spirit moved above;
So later, in the deluge-day,
    Hovered the gentle dove!

"Doves to the sacrificial knife
   The holy Virgin gave;
Her blessed Child's diviner life
   For ends divine to save.

"He rose, baptized on Jordan's shore;
   The Spirit, like a dove,
Hovered while all, transfixed with awe,
   A Voice heard from above!

"For this it is a sacred bird,
   So let it, love, go free;
And listen, if thou ne'er hast heard,
   What it once wrought for *thee*.

"Thou hast forgot that dreary day,
   Some winters now gone past,
When Dachia all expiring lay,
   Each breath might seem the last!

"'Bring, bring the doves, oh, bring them near!'
   The doctor cried in haste—

'Convulsed she lies—I almost fear
   The moment may be past!

"Cover with darkest curtain round,
   Breathe forth the ardent prayer;
Be hushed each vain and worldly sound,
   And bring the pigeons near.'

"We brought the pigeons quickly near,
   My little child revived;
The bird seemed all convulsed with fear,
   It died—my Dachia lived!"

"Oh, mother, had I all this known,
   I ne'er the dove had ta'en;
See, see! already it is flown,
   Already free again!

"And we?—there's nothing left in store,
   Nor cashia, quass, nor meal;
Yet still 'tis better than before,
   Less cold and faint we feel!"

"Thanks for your moral, pretty maid,"
   A stranger voice replied;
"And thanks, fair madame, should be paid
   For teaching sweet supplied."

"A stranger in your land I came,
   Its tongue and lore to learn;
And other lore, by other name,
   I found—'tis now my turn.

"Take this, and fill your empty store
   With cashia, quass, and meal;
And bid the stove give out once more
   The glow you long to feel."

Then homeward wand'ring he thought,
   "How lovely a belief,
So strong, that to a child it brought,
   Mid hunger-pangs, relief.

"How lovely!—that, as Heavenly Love
   Our sorrows bears away,

We on its guileless emblem-dove
   Our mortal pangs may lay!

" In my own land, in days of yore,
   When men both wept and prayed,
This care, when failed their simple lore,
   They oft and oft assayed.

" There was a wisdom in that thought,
   If, amid all their care,
While trembling pigeons near were brought,
   They felt 'The Lord is here!'"

AVIGNON CEMETERY.

Lo! where she rests! beside the flowing Rhône.
Pure spirit! here she gently laid down life,
Here severed the sweet bands of earthly home,
To find a heavenly! Here her cross
Became a palm of victory!—They were
A family of altar-hearts; each wish,
Each passion, offered at the shrine. And e'en
The youngest infants—acolytes—did waft
To heaven the wreathing incense-clouds of prayer.
The one sweet daughter, 'mid that cherub band,
First summoned, in her early promise, died;
The mother next, resigned but stricken, drooped,
Soon followed ; and her deep-eyed fragile boy
Not long survived her.
     A sweet infant pair
Yet lived, the father's heart to charm and soothe;
But in one little week these two were ta'en!
Then quenched were all the fires of love,

And lone, familiar places,—the sweet babes
No more, earth's acolytes, might aid and tend
The household altar-fires—yet burned they still,
Bright with the offerings of Faith and Woe;
And clouds of sweetest incense now became,
As erst the children's prayers—their memory!

VIOLA.

Aug. 3, 1859.

THE FOUNT—SEPARATION.

AMID the deepest, leafiest glades,
    Forth from a rock, in silver jet,
It leapt, a sparkling fount, and played
    Down in a wayward rivulet.

Two children, joyful in its glee,
    Leapt too, and praised the rock, the source:
" Oh, lovely crystal spring! Lo, we
    May join hands o'er its tiny course!"

And down each flower-spangled side,
    They follow, joyous, hand in hand;
Ah me! 'tis getting far too wide,
    Their finger-tips may scarcely blend!

Yet, joyous, laughing, on they press,
    And lightly tread each sandy shore;
Their tones supply the gay caress,
    Their little hands can give no more!

But louder sounds the rolling flood,
    A broken word or two they hear;
Still, eager footsteps print the mud,
    And childish laughter rings out clear!

And now across the reedy banks
    They can but kiss the hand, or wave,
Fond signals meant for love or thanks,
    Like those some parting vessel gave!

And now in vain they strive to see,
    In vain they dash the tears away;
" The stream rolls onward to the sea,
    And we are parted then for aye!"

TOURGUENEV.
(VIOLA, TR.)

THE END.

www.ingramcontent.com/pod-product-compliance
Lightning Source LLC
Chambersburg PA
CBHW031930230426
43672CB00010B/1871